Trade and Security

Trade and Security

U.S. Policies
at Cross-Purposes

Henry R. Nau

The AEI Press

Publisher for the American Enterprise Institute

WASHINGTON, D.C.

1995

AEI is grateful to the Sasakawa Peace Foundation and to the American Express Foundation for their generous support for this project.

Library of Congress Cataloging-in-Publication Data

Nau, Henry R., 1941–
     Trade and security : U.S. policies at cross-purposes / Henry
R. Nau
          p.   cm.
     Includes bibliographical references.

     ISBN 9780-84477-038-3
     1. United States—Commercial policy. 2. United States—Foreign economic relations. 3. United States—Foreign relations—1993–
4. Security, International.   I. American Enterprise Institute. II. Title.
     Hf 1455.N395   1995
     382'.3'0973—dc20   95-39946
                                                                      CIP

1 3 5 7 9 10 8 6 4 2

The AEI Press
Publisher for the American Enterprise Institute
1150 17th Street, N.W., Washington, D.C. 20036

Contents

ACKNOWLEDGMENTS   vii

1   TRADE POLICY ADRIFT   1
    Clinton Administration Trade Policy   3
    Strategic Trade Policy Is Not Strategic   6
    From Cold War to Cold Peace?   9
    A Flawed Trade Policy Vision   12

2   TRADE AND NATIONAL SECURITY   16
    Geo-Economics versus Geopolitics   17
    Politics Won the Cold War   21
    Political Identity and National Security   23

3   SECURITY THREATS AND U.S. TRADE INTERESTS   28
    Continuing Geopolitical Security Threats   28
    Global versus Regional Security and Trade
        Solutions   32
    An EU Trade and Security Bloc   33
    A Japan-centered Asian Security and Trade
        Bloc   36
    A Trade and Security Bloc of the Americas   39
    The Democratic Industrial World—A Global
        Solution   41

4   ALLEGED OBSTACLES TO GLOBAL FREER TRADE   45
    Rival Capitalisms   47
    Changing International Market Conditions   54
    The Asian Development Model   60
    The U.S.-Japan Semiconductor Agreement   67

5 TRADE AND DOMESTIC ECONOMIC POLICIES 71
Embedded Liberalism 72
Export or Trade Pessimism 83

6 AMERICA'S TRADE COMPETITIVENESS SOARS IN THE 1980s 88

7 A BROADER COMPASS FOR U.S. TRADE POLICY 94
Trade and Domestic Values 98
Trade and National Security 100
Trade and Real Bargaining Leverage 103

NOTES 111

ABOUT THE AUTHOR 121

TABLE AND FIGURES
Table 6–1   Manufacturing Productivity in Seven
Industrialized Countries, 1960–1988
and 1992–1993   90
Figure 5–1   Economic Policy and Performance In-
dicators for the United States, 1947–
1992   74
Figure 5–2   Economic Policy and Performance
Incidators for France, Germany,
Japan, and the United Kingdom,
1947–1992   77

Acknowledgments

I wish to thank Claude Barfield and his Project on Technology, Trade, and National Security at the American Enterprise Institute for support of this study. The work is part of a larger book project, tentatively entitled *At Home Abroad: American Foreign Policy in the Twenty-First Century,* sponsored by the Twentieth Century Fund and the Lynde and Harry Bradley Foundation, to be published in 1996.

1

Trade Policy Adrift

The U.S.-Japan auto dispute in the spring of 1995 suggests just how far U.S. trade policy has fallen from the strategic heights of containment and security policy during the cold war. In the auto dispute, U.S. trade policy was stripped of any significance for broader U.S. security and economic policy interests and focused exclusively on promoting exports and jobs in the important but limited automobile sector. For the first time in postwar history, top administration officials actually suggested that this specific trade dispute, if not resolved satisfactorily, could undermine the entire U.S.-Japan security relationship.[1] Not only were U.S. security interests threatened and broader economic problems such as the declining dollar exacerbated by the dispute, but the agreement that ended the dispute yielded less in terms of quantitative results than a comparable automobile dispute when George Bush was president. A *Washington Post* headline summed up the results of the dispute quite well: "A Bitter Fight Produces Little Real Change."[2]

The auto dispute symbolizes a broader transformation of U.S. trade policy that is damaging U.S. foreign policy interests and achieving little in the way of meaningful economic benefits in return. Trade policy has been increasingly isolated from other U.S. foreign policy interests in a

1

single-minded pursuit to capture exports and high-wage jobs for the American economy. The shift has been justified in terms of a new logic of geo-economics and "strategic" trade policy that characterizes a ruthless competition for economic wealth with America's former allies—principally Japan and Germany—in the post–cold war world. The new logic is badly flawed. It causes American policy to ignore real continuing security challenges in the post–cold war world and to expect far too much from trade policy to spur American competitiveness and job growth. It generates endless and escalating disputes with America's friends and undermines collective efforts to deal with America's existing and potential enemies—North Korea, Iran, a resurgent nationalist Russia, and an expanding and assertive China.

Meanwhile, the new policy adds nothing to U.S. competitiveness that has not already been achieved by the dramatic restructuring of American industry through freer trade, competition, and the much greater flexibility of American labor and capital markets. The American-British model of deregulation is at least a decade ahead of the Asian-German model of industrial policy in moving jobs and capital into the information economy.

At the moment, it is not so much what the new U.S. trade policy is doing that is harmful. A tougher-minded trade policy has its place in a new post–cold war U.S. foreign policy. Rather, it is what the new trade policy is not doing that is increasingly damaging. It is not paying enough attention to the big challenges to America's national interests—the economic future of the former Communist countries in Europe and the political stability and security of Asia—and it is forfeiting America's greatest strengths in trade negotiations—its resurgent competitiveness and its capacity on security and broader grounds to mobilize multilateral coalitions against reluctant trade liberalizing countries. A true tough-minded, strategic trade policy would reintegrate trade, economic, and security interests and aim not just at opening foreign markets but at safeguarding these markets against divisive political and security disputes.

Clinton Administration Trade Policy

President Bill Clinton has staked a large part of his foreign policy and domestic economic strategy on U.S. trade policy. For his administration, trade policy is not only the key to U.S. competitiveness and national economic security in a post–cold war world but also the cutting edge of domestic economic reforms that create high-wage jobs and accelerate changes in technology, education, and public infrastructure. This "trade first" strategy has emphasized bilateral, results-oriented negotiations with Japan; regional trade initiatives such as the North American Free Trade Agreement (NAFTA) and the Asian-Pacific Economic Conference (APEC); conclusion of the Uruguay Round (UR) of the General Agreement on Tariffs and Trade (GATT); a national export strategy targeted on the so-called big emerging markets in Asia, the Middle East, southern Africa, and Latin America; and an ambitious national civilian industrial and technology policy under the Advanced Technology Program (ATP) of the Commerce Department.

Despite partial success, President Clinton's trade policy is now drifting and increasingly coming into conflict with larger U.S. security and economic interests. From the beginning, this policy has aimed too low and promised too much. It has focused narrowly on exports to foreign markets but generally ignored more important security and political instabilities in those markets. Geopolitical crises in Bosnia and North Korea, as well as political uncertainty in Mexico, could threaten economic prospects in Europe, Asia, and Latin America. Yet instead of developing comprehensive security and economic policies with European and Asian allies to address these instabilities, the United States targets its allies as new trade adversaries and threats to U.S. national economic security.

3

Similarly, trade policy at home selectively favors a number of high-tech industries and other special interests that seek to increase exports to foreign markets. This policy promises broad benefits for middle-class America; but despite the growing importance of trade in the U.S. economy, trade initiatives are not significant enough to drive economic and technological development. Macroeconomic variables and political confidence remain more important. Thus, partial trade successes, such as NAFTA and the UR, have not arrested continuing domestic discontent. In November 1994, the administration suffered unprecedented setbacks in congressional elections. The new Congress focused on budget issues and denied the president fast-track authority to continue his trade initiatives. The strategy of trade first seemed to have run aground.

In its present form, U.S. trade policy cannot succeed because it is too narrowly conceived. Called a "strategic" trade policy, it is actually divorced from traditional strategic concerns.[3] Trade policy is seen not as a means to confront major geopolitical challenges and opportunities in former cold war adversary states, such as China and Russia, but rather as a tool to grab market share from allied states, such as Germany and Japan. Trade policy is also divorced from broader domestic economic policies. To promote growth, trade depends on sound macroeconomic policies and flexible regulatory policies. For some officials in the Clinton administration, however, trade policy is a substitute for macroeconomic policies and a backdoor to reregulate the economy. While trade deficits linger because of continuing savings and budget deficits, these officials see a so-called strategic trade policy as the new engine of high-wage job and export growth.[4] Trade policy is called on to do more and more, even as it receives less and less support from traditional security and domestic economic policies.

Strategic trade policy assumes that economic competition has replaced geopolitical and military rivalries in the post–cold war world. Nothing could be farther from the truth. Potentially serious threats to U.S. national security exist in Bosnia, North Korea, and Latin America. While none of these problems currently threatens U.S. territory directly, all of them threaten U.S. interests and could undermine foreign export markets. Bosnia is an immediate threat to stability in southern Europe and potentially in central Europe as well. It is also the bellwether of future relations with Russia, the only country in Europe that could significantly harm U.S. security interests. Renewed conflicts with Russia would make it more difficult to deal with ethnic and economic problems throughout the former Communist world from the Adriatic to the Baltic Sea and from Berlin to Moscow. Markets in this region and ultimately in Europe as a whole would suffer. North Korea's paranoia and instability, even if agreements concluded in the fall of 1994 succeed in ending its nuclear weapons program (a *big* if), pose a direct threat to American troops in South Korea; and the looming political transition in Hong Kong and China exposes the weak political foundations of economic expansion in Asia. Haiti, even after the restoration of Aristide, represents Latin America's continued vulnerability to military and authoritarian rule, and the recent financial crisis in Mexico demonstrates the extreme volatility of regional markets and the poor substitute NAFTA is for more stable markets in Europe and Japan.

All these national security threats cry out for cooperation with America's traditional allies in Europe and Japan. Yet U.S. trade policy is on a collision course with these allies. Rather than being a part of a larger national security strategy to deal with instabilities in Europe, Asia, and Latin America, U.S. trade policy increasingly focuses on narrow economic disputes with Europe and Japan and formulates a post-GATT trade round agenda based on environment and labor issues that alienates most of its free market allies in the former Communist countries and developing world.

The point is *not* that specific trade issues with Europe,

Japan, or developing countries are unimportant or that America does not need to be more assertive with its highly competitive allies. The point is rather that current trade policy not only threatens larger U.S. national security interests, but also fails to use larger national security leverage to resolve trade disputes. A larger national security design that emphasized the need to cooperate with allies to facilitate and finance the massive transition toward markets and democracy underway in former Communist and many developing countries would give trade policy a more persuasive rationale. Instead, trade policy becomes increasingly hostage to special interests that care little about national security or, for that matter, comprehensive national economic interests. The standard of trade policy success becomes a cellular telephone agreement with Japan that benefits one American company (the 1993 agreement giving Motorola access to the Nagoya-Tokyo market in Japan), rather than a new post-Uruguay trade round that commits the United States, Japan, and Europe to early integration with reforming countries in the former Communist and developing worlds.

Strategic Trade Policy Is Not Strategic

Clinton's trade policy claims to be "strategic," but it is in fact anything but strategic. So-called strategic trade policy links trade issues to results-oriented, job-creating, and export-sharing agreements in world markets and calls for more interventionist domestic policies to protect and subsidize high-wage, advanced-technology industries. Such a policy is guaranteed to increase tensions with allies and to add to domestic budget and market inflexibilities, carving up static markets rather than creating larger ones. A true strategic trade policy would aim higher: it would entangle Europe and Japan in a broader design, implementing a more assertive U.S. security policy to staunch ethnic chaos in southern Europe and nuclear threats in Asia. It would also draw America's allies into a larger trade initiative that recognizes the vulnerability of regional or bilateral agreements and focuses on a new global round in the World Trade Organization (WTO).

If renegade policies succeed in Bosnia and North Korea, America will ultimately have to spend blood to redeem its security interests in these areas. Why not act more assertively now? Specifically, the United States would seek to link the expansion of NATO to Poland and other countries in central Europe, as well as NATO efforts to prevent the spread of ethnic conflict in Bosnia, with a new U.S.-European economic initiative to strengthen Western markets and open them more aggressively to exports from former Communist countries. The United States would commit forces jointly in areas surrounding Bosnia, such as Macedonia where some U.S. forces already exist; and NATO enlargement to central and Eastern European countries would go hand in hand with new transatlantic trade and economic initiatives suggested by European leaders in the spring of 1995. Similarly, the United States would agree to include China in the new World Trade Organization (favored by Japan and other Asian nations) if Japan and South Korea backed decisive actions to enforce, if necessary, agreements to rid North Korea of nuclear weapons (opposed by Japan and South Korea because of its feared impact on relations with China). This security link is far more acceptable and effective than the links with human rights, because it checks China's military ambitions (by demonstrating U.S.-Japan–South Korean security solidarity) while advancing China's economic interests. Decisive sanctions would make it clear to North Korea and hardline groups in China that "rattling" military threats (for example, Chinese naval threats in the South China Sea) are totally incompatible with the economic aspirations of those countries to join the prosperous world trade and economic system.

Finally, a new trade round premised on larger security interests would offer a more promising direction for Latin American and Caribbean economic growth. Special interests currently oppose freer trade with Latin America and NAFTA enlargement on narrow labor and environmental grounds. Low-wage countries, however, are a greater competitive threat to American jobs in regional than in global markets. A global trade round would not only address political instability in Latin America and other developing areas but also soften and spread the impact of competition from low-wage countries across the markets of all the industrial countries.

This larger design of American national security and trade policy interests would not preclude continued tough bargaining by the United States at the bilateral and regional level. On the contrary, it would aid such bargaining. Right now, U.S. leverage under section 301 and similar trade legislation is confined to cutting off access of other countries to the U.S. market. This policy to deny access is often a bluff because it hurts the United States as much as the targeted country, particularly the strong U.S. industrial interests that depend in many cases on foreign imports. In the context of a larger national security design, the United States would offer something other countries want that also benefits the United States. Japan, for example, gets more predictable trade relations with China, and the United States gets more predictable security arrangements that integrate China more quickly into regional and global markets and alleviate the growing bilateral trade deficit the United States currently incurs with China. Similarly, Europe gets more confident American military leadership, which it wants even though it hates to admit it; and America gets stronger European cooperation to open markets with Eastern Europe and the countries of the former Soviet Union.

Launching a new trade round, however, is impractical as long as confidence lags in domestic economic policies. Thus, trade policy cannot take precedence over correcting fiscal and regulatory policies. Strategic trade policy, which adds trade-related subsidies to budget expenditures and selectively protects home markets, would actually compound the broader economic problem. More free trade, without a decisive step to increase U.S. savings and close the savings-investment deficit (which is the flip side of the current account deficit), would also not help. Trade policy has to be put in perspective: it follows from national security and domestic economic policy objectives. It cannot lead.

President Clinton's trade policy deserves credit for concluding the NAFTA and the GATT negotiations. But premised exclusively on jobs and lacking a larger national security rationale, this policy has paid a higher and higher price in concessions to special interests. Both NAFTA and GATT passed Congress only with debilitating restrictions, including the failure to provide fast-track authority to negotiate further agreements. Lack of such authority could cripple President Clinton's plans to widen the NAFTA and give more substance to APEC. Without it, summit exercises, such as President Clinton attended in Indonesia in November 1994 and the one with Latin American countries in Miami in December 1994, will become increasingly empty. His trade policy, not to mention his total foreign policy, will languish. Clinton's trade policy needs more help from a wider vision of how America and the other industrial nations can go forward from here to stop threats to world peace in Bosnia, North Korea, and Latin America and promote opportunities for democratic transitions in formerly Communist European countries, in Asia, and in the developing world.

From Cold War to Cold Peace?

Two visions compete to guide current U.S. trade policy. One vision grows out of the cold war. It links trade policy to broader national security policy and domestic economic

9

objectives. It is identified with freer trade and traditional domestic policies of price stability and deregulation. During the cold war, American trade policy served American security interests directly. It strengthened the United States and its allies economically in the military struggle against Soviet and Chinese communism. Reciprocal liberalization of trade barriers among the allies enhanced efficiency and helped pay for massive military outlays while also stimulating growth-oriented civilian and commercial investments. For the most part, especially in the 1950s and 1960s, domestic economic policies supported liberalization by upholding stable prices and exchange rates and restraining excessive government regulation and rigidities in the labor and capital markets. In the end, U.S. and Western economic policies, including freer trade, had as much to do with winning the cold war as Western deterrence and alliance policies.[5]

The second vision grows out of post–cold war circumstances. It argues that, with the end of the cold war, the nature of international competition has shifted. Economic warfare has replaced military competition, and a "cold peace" now puts the United States at loggerheads with its industrial allies just as the cold war thrust the United States into military competition with the former Soviet Union.[6] National security policy has to be reconceived to focus on economic security and threats, primarily from former allies but also from newly industrializing countries in Asia and potentially the low-wage countries of Latin America and the developing world.[7] Trade policy is no longer about enhancing common efficiency through trade liberalization and lower prices but grabbing market share and intervening through government subsidies and protection to aid specifically American-owned firms and investment, especially in high-wage, high-tech sectors.[8] It is identified with strategic planning but not of the geopolitical sort that guided U.S. policies in the cold war. National strategy is now more like that of a multinational firm competing in world markets for sales and jobs.[9] According to this post–cold war doctrine of trade policy, the United States must redirect its national security policies to boost American exports in global markets and demand that other countries, particularly low-wage transition and developing countries, raise their labor, safety, and environmental standards before they trade in U.S. markets.

Clinton administration policies up to this point have tried to straddle these two visions. On the one hand, President Clinton emphasizes the need to compete, not retreat, in world markets. He advocates a tough-minded, results-oriented trade policy to achieve market-opening objectives in Japan and within regional communities in Latin America (NAFTA) and the Far East (APEC). He sees these initiatives as consistent with GATT and, at the G-7 summit in Naples, Italy, in July 1994, issued a call for a new post–Uruguay Trade Round, even before the Uruguay Round agreement was ratified by Congress in November 1994. On the other hand, many of his administration officials and supporters in Congress are convinced that freer trade is no longer in America's interests. They advocate bilateral and regional initiatives for their own sake or as alternatives to GATT, and they propose a quantitative or quota-based approach to international trade that would divide up export markets on the basis of strict product or sector reciprocity and expand domestic government intervention to allocate not only research and development subsidies to high-tech industries but also investment capital for manufacturing and marketing activities.[10]

The battle between these two visions in the Clinton administration is coming to a head. Passage of the NAFTA and GATT agreements was more difficult than any previous trade legislation, and passage of future trade agreements, particularly if fast-track authority is included, will be more difficult than NAFTA or GATT. The reason is simple: the post–cold war strategic trade vision is too limited and defensive. Each trade agreement pays a higher debt than the last one to special interests. Compromises to pass NAFTA (for example, to textile producers in the Caribbean) return to impede passage of GATT. Passage of GATT saddles future trade negotiations with restrictive labor and environmental provisions. Advocates of broader national interests fall farther and farther behind.

Unless the Clinton administration reconceives trade policy and links it with broader national security and domestic economic interests, America's trade prospects will shrink. So too will prospects for American jobs and economic growth. Ultimately, prospects for the Clinton administration, which has staked its future on trade and economic policy, will also shrink.

A Flawed Trade Policy Vision

The vision of America's national interests contained in the strategic trade policy approach is flawed. Its logic falls short in three areas:

- It never spells out the military or geopolitical threats that a tougher national economic security policy is designed to serve. In effect, the strategic trade vision depends on a post–cold war world in which fewer military threats exist even as it uses trade policy to wage economic warfare and create potentially new military threats.
- Rather than supplement domestic growth, strategic trade policy actually works against it. Interventionist industrial and high-tech policies, designed to grab export jobs and market shares, increase budget outlays and the share of labor and capital resources directly allocated by government—both of which weaken domestic markets and growth.
- The strategic trade policy vision completely underestimates the growing worldwide emphasis on free market policies and the new competitiveness of American industry gained through traditional monetary and investment

policies in the 1980s. Instead, it exalts an alternative model of economic competitiveness, identified with Japan and the Asian newly industrializing countries (NICs), that features mercantilist trade policies and authoritarian, anticonsumer domestic policies.[11]

Strategic trade doctrine sees Asian capitalism as a "third way" between American capitalism and the discredited Socialist dogma. Regrettably, it ignores the fact that *Asian capitalism succeeded only in the context of American capitalism.* American capitalism created the open, competitive international markets that provided the opportunities and signals for government-directed capitalism in Japan and the Asian NICs. Without global freer trade, the Asian model of capitalism would have fared no better than the Socialist model of the former Communist countries or the fascist model of South Africa.

The rest of this volume explores these flaws in strategic trade policy theology. It shows that national goals are not just about military security or economic security but about defining and defending a vision of America that promotes individual freedom and opportunity. For the first time ever in the post–cold war world, America shares a basic liberal vision of freedom and markets with a wider group of nations, including all industrial nations and many industrializing ones as well. These countries pose absolutely no military threat to the United States. So-called rival capitalisms among these nations are not to be confused with the rival nationalisms of the 1930s.[12] Nor are trade disputes to be confused with economic warfare or national security.[13] America's real security interests continue to focus on China, Russia, and the Middle East, not on rivalries with America's democratic allies or low-wage developing nations.

Russia and China remain the only two nuclear powers that can directly harm the United States. Russia, its transition to democracy, and its relations with countries in central and Eastern Europe, the Baltic region, the Middle East, the Caucasus, and south central Asia define one axis of instability and potential danger for American interests. China, its leadership after Deng, and its relations with Hong Kong, Taiwan, the two Koreas, Japan, and the rest of north and Southeast Asia define the other. If democracy fails in Eastern Europe and the former Soviet republics or if authoritarianism and fundamentalism prevail in Asia and the Middle East, America once again faces direct military threats to its national security. Arms races driven by virulent nationalism, nuclear terrorism, massive refugee movements, and environmental havoc will quickly descend on America's doorsteps. Fostering stability and prosperity in former Communist and developing areas, therefore, is crucial to American interests.

To establish stability and prosperity in former Communist and authoritarian countries, America cannot go it alone. Its security and economic ties with Europe and Japan remain paramount. The end of the cold war has not altered the requirement for NATO or the U.S.-Japan Security Treaty, as we painfully observe today in Bosnia and on the Korean peninsula. Nor has it ended or even reduced the urgency of open markets and global economic ties with Europe and Japan. Alone or within regional blocs only, none of the allies can afford the cost of promoting democracy and markets in the former Communist and authoritarian world. U.S. regional markets in Latin America or Asia can never substitute for more massive European markets, especially if Eastern Europe and the former Soviet republics grow. Even if regional markets in the Americas and Asia expand, this outcome will do little to stem the threat of political instability in Europe, the Balkans, the Caucasus, or the Middle East. Economic regionalism potentially excludes the United States from Europe, where the United States retains essential security interests. It also stakes America's future on less stable markets in Asia. The political and security basis of a Japan- or China-centered system in Asia is much weaker than a European Union–centered system in Europe. Trade regionalism, in short, would be a disaster for America's security interests and would diminish America's economic prospects as well.

What is more, there is no need to retreat to regionalism. American industry is much more competitive than declinists or strategic trade policy advocates suggest. The World Competitiveness Report for 1994, issued by the Swiss-based International Institute for Management Development and the World Economic Forum, placed the United States once again at the top of the list of most competitive economies. The United States regained the lead from Japan for the first time since 1985.[14] Recent studies document a remarkable comeback of American productivity and exports since the mid-1980s, largely on the strength of traditional policies of monetary restraint and deregulation rather than industrial and technology innovation policies championed by strategic trade policy advocates.[15] While American industry faces stiff competition in Europe and Japan and cannot become complacent again, it also need not fear global freer trade or assume that an Asian model of development and inherent advantages of low-wage countries are inevitably superior to the Anglo-American model of industrial development. Conditions in international markets do not suggest a growing role of oligopolistic competition and the obsolescence of freer trade. If anything, international markets are more competitive today than immediately after World War II when U.S. companies dominated international commerce. In such markets, more prudent fiscal policies in the United States, like those in Japan and Germany during much of the postwar period, would probably do more to reduce trade imbalances and restore the mutual benefits of freer trade than adopting some of the more objectionable anticonsumer and collusive technocratic policies of such rivals as Japan.

2

Trade and National Security

The new strategic trade doctrine separates trade policy from military and security policy. In so doing, it assumes a very contradictory set of conditions about world security affairs. On the one hand, the doctrine argues that there are no serious geopolitical or military threats to American security. The end of the cold war, it is said, makes it possible for the United States to rely less on its allies and to compete with them more blatantly and aggressively on trade and economic issues. Yet, at the same time, the doctrine assumes that this economic competition is so intense and apparently so similar to traditional military competition that the United States cannot afford to depend on any of its allies for important defense technology. Any challenge to America's economic competitiveness or independent defense industrial base becomes a threat to America's national security, even though it is completely unclear from strategic trade doctrine who the enemy is or indeed if there is a serious adversary at all since America needs no allies. National security is reduced to "powernomics," the pursuit of wealth and power, markets and jobs for their own sake. Powernomics in turn approaches paranoia, the avoidance of any defense technology dependence, not to defend against a specific national security threat, but apparently to defend against all possible threats in a world of reduced threats.[1] National security becomes the equivalent of a finely tuned athlete who offers no quarter to opponents but has no specific opponent to confront.

Geo-Economics versus Geopolitics

The confusion stems from a broader misunderstanding that afflicts post–cold war discussions of American foreign policy.

A new axiom of post–cold war diplomacy is that economic power and competition have replaced traditional military rivalries. Geo-economics, not geopolitics, decides the winners and losers of the new era.[2] New trading states, it is argued, are concerned not with the defense of territory but with the defense of jobs and the conquest of world markets.[3] From this perspective, trade has little to do with traditional objectives of strengthening allies and denying critical technologies to military rivals; it has to do rather with securing jobs and warding off threats to America's economic security from friendly or hostile states, primarily from predatory countries such as Japan or low-wage production havens such as Mexico. Trade policy, in short, has been ripped out of the context of "high politics" calculations based on strategic and geopolitical factors and linked up with low politics or the specific job and production requirements of individual firms and industries. To complete the inversion of traditional thinking, trade policy becomes "strategic," while "strategic" in the old sense becomes extinct.

There is, of course, some truth to the observation that military power is not the immediate preoccupation or determinant of national security policy that it was in the cold war struggle between the two nuclear superpowers. And there is further truth to the claim that economic competition has intensified among the former cold war allies or Western industrial nations. But the statement that economic competition has replaced military power is misleading, if not plain false. It is not sustained even by its advocates. As I have already pointed out, strategic trade policy analysts worry mindlessly about economic and technological dependence, even though they insist that America faces no strategic rivals and therefore needs no military allies. If economic competition were "deadly" serious, America would need allies and would be looking for ways to strengthen collective military strength with allies through military research and development cooperation and weapons codevelopment and coproduction. True, cooperating with allies in defense areas increases interdependence. At the margins, American military leaders may worry about getting critical defense technologies from their allies. But this concern becomes serious only if allies sharply disagree with the United States about the broad security issues facing the industrialized democracies.

Does Japan entertain sharply different national security interests from those of the United States, interests that might lead Japan to deny the United States critical defense technologies? To be sure, some outspoken nationalists in Japan have suggested as much,[4] and some studies claim that Japanese firms are refusing to supply American high-technology companies with their latest and best technologies or do so only with a delay.[5] But extreme nationalists do not currently control the Japanese government, and Japanese companies do not currently deny the United States technologies that they systematically supply to America's enemies. If the United States believes such prospects are imminent, then it should not argue that economic competition has replaced military competition but gear up to confront Japanese nationalists as serious military adversaries. Strategic trade studies should identify the areas in which U.S. and Japanese security interests sharply diverge and the direct or third-party conflicts (for example, Russia, North Korea, and so forth) in which the Japanese might deny the United States needed defense technologies. Such studies would not show sharp differences.

How likely is it that Japan or any other ally would act against significant U.S. interests in the post–cold war world? Japan still depends totally on the United States for its security and, as I note later, is unlikely to develop a non-U.S.-Japan-centered security system in Asia. How likely is it that the United States would take significant actions without the support of its allies? The rule of thumb in practically all conflicts since the fall of the Berlin Wall—Kuwait, Bosnia, North Korea, and Haiti—is that the United States acts only under the auspices of NATO or the United Nations. If it had to act alone frequently, against opposition from its allies, the very premise of strategic trade arguments that military competition has subsided would be invalidated.

Thus, a plausible response to technological interdependence in the post–cold war world would be to buy some insurance against the very low probability that the United States may have to act alone, but not to pay too much for this insurance. A new government bureaucracy to monitor and implement a competitiveness-oriented industrial policy[6] or a new trade policy of "sophisticated neomercantilism" seems too high a price to pay.[7] The best insurance policy would seem to be to promote selective, cross-cutting transnational cooperation and integration of defense and commercial capabilities in critical dual-use technologies, ensuring that all democratic countries depend to some extent on one another for crucial defense needs.[8] This is the strategy of so-called strategic alliances that transnational corporations pursue in commercial markets to keep abreast of new technologies abroad without trying to be fully independent in each of those technologies.

Economic competition among democratic nations, then, is not an equivalent or substitute for traditional military rivalries. It is, in fact, a much milder form of rivalry. Economic competition, in terms of daily rivalries among numerous companies, emerges in intense fashion only where political differences have narrowed to the point that military rivalries have become unthinkable. Historically, economic competition has always been much greater within domestic than international markets, and among friends rather than between adversaries. Intense trade takes place within political communities, not in the absence of such communities.

What has led to the massive and highly competitive markets among industrial countries in the post–cold war world, then, is not just the disappearance of military rivalries among these countries but also the flip side of this phenomenon, the growth of a closer political community among nations that share basic democratic political values and market-oriented economic practices. The twenty-four industrial member nations of the Organization for Economic Cooperation and Development (which now also includes Mexico, a twenty-fifth member) are all open, market-oriented, democratic societies that settle internal disputes through peaceful, noncoercive means. What is even more interesting is that these societies also tend to resolve *external* disputes among themselves through peaceful, nonmilitary means. Historically, they have rarely, if ever, fought wars against one another, although they do fight wars against nondemocratic societies as often as the latter have fought wars among themselves. The evidence of this fact in studies of hundreds of conflicts among hundreds of countries, both democratic and nondemocratic, is startling.[9] Democratic nations not only do not fight wars with one another, but they do not escalate disputes to the military level. They resolve those disputes short of military threats through diplomatic and civil means, allowing issues including commercial issues to be resolved by courts and administrative procedures.

In an important sense, the industrial nations already constitute a single democratic civil society or community in which major political or geopolitical conflicts do not exist. No industrial nation has a territorial dispute with any other, and none arms against or threatens another militarily or even thinks about doing so.[10] This political reality lies behind the disappearance of military conflict and the rise of economic competition among industrial nations. And it could potentially extend to previously nondemocratic states in the former Communist and developing worlds. Trade competition in this context is not a new source of strategic rivalry; it is the replacement of military rivalries by civil societies that eschew military means and embrace common political and judicial procedures to resolve commercial and other disputes.

Politics Won the Cold War

What has changed in the post–cold war world, therefore, is not the mysterious replacement of military by economic power, or geopolitics by geo-economics, but the emergence of a community or zone of democratic peace among industrial nations.[11] This change has come about not suddenly since the end of the cold war but over the "long peace"[12] of the cold war in which both military and economic competition played a role. The cold war was not decided alone or primarily by military competition. To be sure, the United States and the Soviet Union competed militarily and eventually achieved a military balance, including nuclear and conventional capabilities, that checkmated military aggression, most importantly in central Europe. But military power was not the decisive determinant of the outcome of this competition. Economic power was at least as important. Geo-economics is not something new. It has always been there, and it helped to decide the cold war.[13]

At the end of the cold war, the Soviet Union was stronger militarily than it was at the beginning of the cold war. A massive buildup of military power in the 1960s and 1970s enabled it to rival the United States as a nuclear superpower. In 1991, when the Soviet Union collapsed, its military muscle bristled. Why didn't the Soviet Union strike to preserve its empire in central Europe? The answer is a mystery to conventional postwar American foreign policy thinking. Realism, the international relations theory underlying containment, has no answer. Countries are not supposed to relinquish power without a fight.[14] In fact, historically, growing equality, such as the Soviet Union enjoyed with the United States at the military level, is supposed to be destabilizing and lead to war.[15] Realism predicts that the Soviet Union would fight. Maybe nuclear weapons deterred the Soviet Union from striking because war now meant self-destruction. But the Soviet Union did not need to use nuclear weapons to protect its empire in Europe. A crackdown with conventional forces would have sufficed, and the West was unlikely to have intervened. Still the Soviet Union did not try to save itself. Why?

The answers lie in political and economic competition between the United States and the Soviet Union. While Soviet military muscle bristled, its economic muscle atrophied. Its industries, saturated by the cholesterol of easy credit and immobile labor, died of hardening of the arteries; and its economic system, strangled by the centralized creed of state ownership and direction, went comatose in the face of the information revolution and the fast pace of innovation and corporate change. With its economic heart in seizure, the Soviet Union's military muscle ultimately mattered little.

Still the Soviet Union might have struck, despite its struggling economy. Indeed, a military thrust might have revived its economic prospects, at least in the short term. But it surrendered rather than fight. It had lost its political will to continue. In the end, the political competition decided the cold war. What changed was not just the collapse of the Soviet economic system but a shattering of the Soviet Union's political self-image. The Soviet leadership and many of its people no longer believed in the system. They no longer identified with the Soviet empire or with communism. They wanted to change their political beliefs.

Today, Russia is shaping a new national image or identity (as are other former Soviet republics and satellite countries). It is demonstrating that, at the core of international politics and conflict, lies the political identity of individual nations. This identity, whether democratic, totalitarian, or something in between, provides the purpose and the will to acquire and use economic and military power. National security does not originate in military power or economic wealth. It originates in how a society conceives of itself and, most important, how it organizes its political institutions to guide the acquisition and use of economic and military power. National security is about domestic politics long before it is about how to secure domestic politics from foreign threats (that is, geopolitics) or how to make the domestic economy grow and take advantage of the international economy (that is, geo-economics). If the end of the cold war has done anything, it has lifted the veil that obscured the relationship between domestic politics on the one hand and international economic and military affairs on the other.[16]

Political Identity and National Security

Political identity is the starting point from which the United States has to rethink the relationship between trade policy and national security in the post–cold war world. It is a starting point that should be congenial to the Clinton administration with its emphasis on domestic policy. Yet the president seems locked into the traditional tendency to see domestic and foreign affairs as being in conflict with one another. He *reluctantly* spends time on foreign affairs because he promised the electorate he would focus on domestic affairs; and while he talks about the importance of a strong domestic economy for foreign policy, he fails to link this domestic vision with common goals among democratic nations. Many of his supporters viscerally oppose freer trade, without recognizing that protectionism implies not only a weaker industrial-nation community vis-à-vis continuing security risks in former Communist and authoritarian nations but also a meaner, more divided, and less tolerant

American society at home. Trade barriers discriminate among American citizens at home as well as against foreign citizens abroad.

Seen from a perspective that integrates domestic and foreign affairs, trade and economic policy is not an instrument of powernomics; rather it reflects and reinforces the political identity or purposes of a society or group of societies. In this sense, freer trade in the cold war period was not just a policy to maximize Western economic strength in the military competition with the Soviet Union. It was also a means to express and build open societies. It reflected the internal imperative of democratic societies to find peaceful ways to resolve ethnic and national divisions (for example, as France and Germany did, ending centuries of rivalry) and to nurture the transition from authoritarian to democratic traditions through private commerce (for example, as freer trade did during the cold war, bringing Japan, Germany, Spain, Portugal, and Greece into the society of democratic nations). Realist perspectives like to argue that freer trade emerged after World War II because the United States was the dominant power and had the most to gain from freer trade.[17] If this were so, however, the Soviet Union, which was also dominant in its part of the world, would have adopted freer trade policies among the Warsaw Pact countries. It did not because such an external policy would have been totally inconsistent with its internal identity. Nations do not formulate foreign policies only or primarily on the basis of relative external wealth and power. They also do so on the basis of their internal beliefs and domestic practices.

Identity and self-image raise questions of national purpose and political philosophy, without which it is difficult to know what a country's national interests are.[18] Unless national interests are reduced to pure material power and geography, these interests involve values that define the political community that occupies a particular piece of geography and tells us for what purposes and ideas that country will develop and employ its material (economic and military) power. It is not in America's national interests or a requirement of national sovereignty to oppose foreign investment or participation in international organizations when that foreign investment comes from countries that share democratic values or those international organizations have memberships that are wholly or largely democratic. America does not exist for its own sake; it exists to promote individual liberty and economic opportunity. If it can do that more effectively by sharing some sovereignty and pooling efforts with like-minded countries, it should do so. The protection of private rights and the promotion of public participation in decisionmaking are the hallmarks of the American nation, not the defense of some materialistic geographic space or the maintenance of sovereignty and independence for their own sake.

An identity perspective reconstructs the relationship between U.S. trade and national security policy in three steps. The first step is to determine what nations pose an existing or potential threat to the United States in the post–cold war world. Such nations need not only to possess significant economic or military power but also to be inclined to use this power for political purposes antithetical to America's self-image or to the self-image of the democratic community with which America identifies around the world. This question actually breaks down into two parts: (1) what are the continuing political conflicts and risks to American security interests outside the democratic world in the areas demarcated by the former Soviet empire in Europe, China in the Far East, and conflicts in the Middle East? and (2) are these conflicts and risks likely to be assessed so differently by other democratic nations that significant gaps may reemerge between the self-images of the United States and those of other democratic nations, eventually recreating national security rivalries among democratic nations?

If the answer to the second question is no, the second step in reconstructing national security policy in the post–cold war world is to build on the common political values of the democratic nations and design trade and economic policies that serve the interests of all free nations. Is freer trade at the global level still the best policy for defending the freedom and promoting the growth and jobs of both the United States and its friends? Or have world market conditions changed in such a way that strategic trade policy offers a better alternative and that the Asian model of development is inherently superior under modern circumstances to traditional neoclassical economics? For the United States to compete in more intensely competitive, oligopolistic global markets, is it necessary to go beyond the role of government prescribed in neoclassical economics? Neoclassical economics foresees a role for government in protecting private property, managing fiscal and monetary policies, and enforcing antitrust and competition policies. Strategic trade goes further and adopts more pervasive direct intervention on the part of government to create new technologies and industries and support their conquest of domestic and foreign markets. An assessment of these questions suggests that freer trade is far from obsolete.

If freer trade and neoclassical economics remain the better policy, the third step is to reintegrate trade policy with the real national security interests of the United States and the democratic world. What, in short, is an alternative trade and national security strategy to the so-called strategic trade and national economic security policy that is gaining dominance in the Clinton administration? Can America bargain hard with Japan and Europe for bigger stakes than narrow product and sector-specific agreements such as the U.S.-Japan semiconductor agreement and the Motorola cellular telephone agreement? Can the United States nurture domestic political and market reforms in developing countries without denying them their comparative advantages and requiring them to meet immediately the labor, social, and environmental standards of developed nations?

The next three chapters take up those steps toward reconstructing a post–cold war U.S. trade policy that is truly strategic.

3

Security Threats and U.S.
Trade Interests

Bosnia, North Korea, and political instabilities in Haiti and, in a milder sense, in Mexico are the most serious *potential* threats to U.S. national security. None of these conflicts is currently an *actual* or even a serious threat. Direct or urgent intervention of American forces is probably not warranted, although American forces are already at risk in Macedonia, South Korea, and Haiti. To say this, however, is not to conclude that American security interests are not at stake. A threat is not something that is either on or off. It develops or recedes gradually. What we see in these three situations is the potential for three more serious conflicts that directly affect America's security—conflicts with Russia, tensions with China, and floods of refugees on America's immediate southern borders.

Continuing Geopolitical Security Threats

Bosnia reflects the economic and political ruin left in Europe by decades of communism. Communism repressed political conflict by force and did little to raise economic standards to promote tolerance. It left the raw material for violence in practically all former Communist countries, as well as between some of them (for example, Ukraine and Russia). Violence in any one or several of these countries is unavoidable and already exists in Bosnia, Armenia, Azerbaijian, Georgia, Tajikistan, and Moldova. Up to a certain level, such violence does not seriously threaten U.S. or even European interests. At a level where it reverses prospects for political and economic reforms in the former Communist countries, however, especially Russia, it becomes a threat. Under such circumstances, Russia is likely to rearm, exert a more aggressive policy toward neighboring former republics such as Ukraine, escalate Russian intervention in the Caucasus and south central Asia, and trigger renewed tensions in places such as the former Yugoslavia and the Baltic States. A European Union would be a poor substitute for NATO to counter revived Russian aggression. The United States will have to be involved or abandon its interests in Europe to a weak and divided European security community.

What is more, America is already involved and getting involved more deeply. The United States has decided to expand NATO to protect the central European countries (Hungary, Poland, the Czech Republic, and Slovakia) from potential ethnic or external threats. NATO is conducting a study in 1995 to determine when and how to carry out this expansion. Hungary borders on Serbia. Thus, any expansion of the conflict in the former Yugoslavia directly threatens countries that are, deliberately but nevertheless decisively, being brought into the Western alliance. Indifference to the spread of violence in the Balkans, therefore, is not possible if the United States is serious about its larger defense objectives in the whole of Europe.

North Korea is the most immediate threat to American security interests because American troops guard the frontier in South Korea. The outbreak of hostilities instantly involves America in another land war in Asia, as costly as, if not more costly than, the earlier Korean and Vietnam Wars. But even if it does not lead to war, the North Korean threat exposes the weak political foundations of economic and military relations in Asia. North Korean nuclear diplomacy threatens Japan. While Japan does not say today that it would respond by developing its own nuclear weapons, Japan would clearly depend more than ever before on U.S. weapons. This dependence would strain U.S.-Japanese alliance relations, committing the United States to continue to defend a wealthy allied nation and escalating painful burdens of psychological and political dependence in Japan. If American guarantees should weaken, Japan would face momentous domestic as well as regional choices. Any remilitarization or nuclearization of Japan would have vast and no doubt dire consequences for Japan's relations with all other countries in the region, especially China. China opposes nuclear weapons in North Korea but also resists a firm cooperative policy to enforce a no-nuclear policy on the Pyongyang regime. Some hard-liners in China may see some benefits in North Korean policies as a means to balance U.S. and Japanese pretensions in the region. China is not sufficiently open for the United States and other countries to know exactly what Chinese intentions are in North Korea or elsewhere. A domestic transition is underway to succeed Deng Xiaoping, the aging Chinese leader, and Chinese policies could become more unpredictable as hard-liners and others vie to influence such explosive issues as the transition in Hong Kong (due to be transferred from British to Chinese sovereignty in 1997) and the rivalry for oil resources in the South China Sea (where Chinese naval vessels have already attacked other countries' vessels in disputes over energy resources in the Spratly Islands). China is a nuclear power and has been increasing its military expenditures significantly in recent years.[1] In short, the political and security situation in Asia is fragile, particularly if the United States and Japan have a serious falling out over trade issues. North Korea may be only the tip of the iceberg.

Among the three threats considered here, Haiti is perhaps the least urgent in military terms. But it reflects the kind of problem that American security confronts throughout the developing world. Left unattended, political instability in the Caribbean, Mexico, Central America, Africa, and the Middle East could lead to massive refugee and immigration movements, television spectacles of mass starvation and murder, and escalating terrorist, drug-trafficking, and environmental threats. Mexico is a special case. It has a relatively strong developing economy and coherent political society. But it is undergoing significant economic and political change, and it will experience periodic reverses as it did in late 1994 and early 1995. The future of America's southern border areas will be affected regardless of what America does.

Neither Mexico, Haiti, nor any of the developing countries to the south poses a military threat to the United States, as would a resurgent nationalist Russia or a militarily strong China. Even the refugee, terrorist, drug, and environmental threats are not sufficient in their present dimensions to pose a dire physical threat to the United States. The threat to the United States in these cases is not power; it is in fact the lack of power, the destitution, the human savagery, and the loss of meaning of life itself that not only undermines the stability of countries abroad but also clouds and contaminates America's sense of purpose at home. The threat, in short, is to America's self-image.

America cannot develop and retain a credible multicultural political image and society at home if it callously dismisses the loss of human life abroad, especially in developing countries from which the minority population of America, almost one-third of the U.S. population, draws its historical and cultural heritage. Black Americans, for example, led the campaign to intervene in Haiti. By the same token, however, a self-image of concern also dictates caution. In the Vietnam War, America pursued a self-image of defending freedom so vigorously that, for many Americans, that self-image became one of unrestrained coercion that they could no longer accept. Foreign policy is always an effort to integrate values and power. The col-

31

lapse of the Soviet Union reminds us that this integration can be lost at home; Vietnam reminds us that it can be lost abroad. The essential element of any nation's life is that it feels proud and good about what it uses its military power and economic wealth for, both at home and abroad.

Global versus Regional Security and Trade Solutions

How does the United States respond to these post–cold war security threats? As long as the problems are not immediate (and, as I have argued, except for the threat to American forces in South Korea, none of these problems is urgent in the same sense as the presence of Soviet forces in central Europe was during the cold war), can and should the United States leave the problems to its newly wealthy and powerful allies—Europe and Japan? Is not Bosnia primarily a European problem and North Korea a Japanese one? Many strategic trade policy advocates want Europe and Japan to resume full responsibility for their own security problems. During the cold war, as they see it, the United States paid the lion's share of defense costs, and the allies stole an economic advantage on the United States by devoting more resources to commercial objectives. Now, with the cold war over, the allies can become more normal countries and tend to their own security problems.[2]

Fair enough. The problems in Europe and Asia, leave aside for the moment problems in the Caribbean and Latin America, are in the first instance security problems for the allies. The next question should be, however, whether the allies can handle these problems either alone or on the basis of regional solutions that significantly reduce American responsibilities. Do not forget, as we have just discussed, American interests too are involved in these areas. Purely commercial strategic trade policy considerations may dictate letting the allies wrestle with their own problems, but true strategic policy consideration requires thinking through whether the allies can actually manage these problems alone. If they cannot and America does nothing, America will sacrifice critical national security interests in both Europe and Asia.

For the United States, with essential interests outside the Western Hemisphere, regional security solutions are nonstarters. As the rest of this chapter details, regional conflicts in Europe and Asia are not likely to be successfully contained on a regional basis alone. And, while the United States may be able to manage regional conflicts in the Western Hemisphere by itself, a Western Hemispheric community cannot ensure U.S. national security interests in Europe and Asia. Even in the post–cold war world, America is "doomed" to global solutions for its true strategic interests.

This being the case, regional trade solutions are also nonstarters.[3] Like the proverbial fruit from the tree, trade never falls far from the branches of political alliances or community. Markets grow where security and trust exist, not where anarchy and animosity prevail. Strategic trade advocates, who prefer regional or bilateral trade solutions over global ones, never examine the actual strategic conditions that might or might not support stable trade relations. If they did, they would find regional markets much less favorable than global ones.

Let's look at the prospects for security and trade communities in the major regions—Europe under German or EU leadership, Asia under Japanese leadership, and the Western Hemisphere under American leadership.

An EU Trade and Security Bloc

Can the European Union manage alone and successfully the unprecedented transition going on in the former Communist world in Eastern Europe and the old Soviet republics? The political requirements are staggering. Everyone agrees that the former Communist Europe cannot reform without some sense of security against violent border changes, resurgent ethnic and nationalist antagonisms, the proliferation of conventional and nuclear arms, and resulting arms races. Are the Western European Union (WEU), the nascent military arm of Europe, and the common European security and foreign policy community, ordained by the Maastricht Treaty in 1991, up to the task?[4] As the EU's experience in the former Yugoslavia suggests, it is doubtful. The Maastricht Treaty itself did not envision a solo role for Europe. It stated that the WEU would be developed both "as the defense component of the European Union *and* as the means to strengthen the European pillar of the Atlantic Alliance" (emphasis added). More recently, the German and French defense ministers and other European leaders have talked about a new transatlantic contract or covenant to revitalize security and economic ties with the United States before the European Union reviews the Maastricht Treaty at the Intergovernmental Conference scheduled for 1996.[5] To be sure, there are differences among the Atlantic countries over how strong the European pillar should be and whether a European pillar strengthens American commitments to Europe or weakens them and encourages American unilateralism. In the future, some Europeans and some Americans may be tempted to conclude that Europe could handle post–cold war security responsibilities without the United States. Such a conclusion, however, while possible, would be foolhardy. The reasons become clear when one considers more fundamental differences among Western European powers.

Germany is a nonnuclear power. Unless nuclear diplomacy has been permanently banished from future international relations under all circumstances, a highly dubious proposition, on whom does Germany rely for nuclear protection in the event of a resurgent nationalism in Russia or the spread of nuclear weapons to Ukraine (should Ukraine fail to complete the transfer of such weapons to Russia or reacquire these weapons on its own thereafter)? Consider the same question in the case of a buildup

of conventional arms in the former Communist Europe—
Ukraine arming against a resurgent Russia, or Poland
against Ukraine or against Russia if Russia begins to reas-
sert influence once again in Ukraine? To whom does Germany turn for help? Itself? There are those who see an
independent German nuclear and military force as a sta-
bilizing factor in Europe's future.[6] But this optimistic view
does not seem to be shared by the policy makers and citizens of the countries most directly involved in the issue.
No country in Europe favors a German nuclear role, and
no alternative to NATO is evident or likely. Is a French-
British–led nuclear or a French-German–led conventional
force (the "Euro-corps") an alternative? Germany has always said no to the first, not without the U.S. nuclear um-
brella, and no to the second, not without a European force
as part of, rather than a substitute for, NATO (its view on
the Euro-corps). The European Union may well, over a
lengthy period of time, develop a common security force
and policy and a capacity to act outside Europe if necessary without the United States (the purpose of WEU forces
that might be tasked independently of NATO). But it is
not likely to develop a fully independent, alternative policy
to NATO for central conflicts inside Europe. This is a conclusion, by the way, that follows strictly from the preferences of Germany and other European states, not because
U.S. national security interests require NATO and a continuing U.S. role in Europe.[7]

To reform successfully, the former Communist Europe needs not only a sense of security but also aid and
trade. Can the European Community meet these costs on
its own, without U.S. or Japanese participation? Again,
the answer seems to be no. Germany is spending approxi-
mately $100 billion a year in the former East Germany alone
to restructure a society of 16 million people and an
economy with a gross domestic product (GDP) of approxi-
mately $150 billion. Even if nothing close to that is antici-
pated on a proportional scale for the rest of former

Communist Europe, which has 400 million people and an economy of $1.5 trillion, the costs are monumental. (For Russia alone, the West has already committed though not fully spent $10-15 billion a year and is not seeing much progress.) In the short term, certainly, Germany and the rest of Europe cannot handle the cost.[8] So one consequence of a European regional solution to the problems of transition in former Communist countries will be a much slower process of reform in the East—one country or small region (such as the former East Germany) at a time. A slower pace increases the chances of conflict and setback in the region and hence exacerbates the security problem. In this scenario, Europe would face such problems largely on its own.

Trade with the East on a Europe-only basis would probably be just as indigestible as the large requirements for aid. Afraid of low-wage competitors, the EU is already reluctant to open its markets for Eastern products, particularly the products the East exports competitively—steel, agriculture, textiles, and the like. These are the same sectors that the EU jealously protects. Moreover, with its own unemployment problems and Germany's preoccupation with absorbing former East Germany, Europe has little money left over for investment in the East. The leading investor in the former Communist countries in the early 1990s was the United States.[9] With slower access to investment capital and markets, unemployment in the East will persist and likely increase, and immigration will intensify. Given attitudes toward foreigners in Western Europe and legacies in Germany limiting citizenship to immigrants with German blood, Western Europe is not in a particularly good position to manage this problem effectively.[10]

A Japan-centered Asian Security and Trade Bloc

What about Japan as the leader of a new political community and trading bloc in Asia? This possibility is even less feasible than that of a European bloc (despite the optimistic appraisals of some strategic trade advocates, who do not really consider strategic issues).[11] Political community has always been weaker in Asia than in Europe. Because of Japan's more glacial recognition of its wartime responsibilities (changing somewhat under recent Japanese governments) and its intrinsically insular and homogeneous social attitudes, Japan is politically suspect in the region, even as a junior partner with the United States. Hence whatever community exists in Asia, it is based on a predominant U.S. political and security presence in the region (for which Japan is no substitute) and a parallel presence of U.S. and Japanese trade and economic interests among the diverse and sometimes antagonistic countries of East and Southeast Asia.

It is true, as President Clinton noted at APEC in Seattle in November 1993, that security in Asia has improved and that many of these countries have gone from being "dominoes" in the great power struggle of the cold war to being "dynamos" in world economic growth.[12] But many of these countries are in political transition or are still authoritarian. The openness of domestic political processes and markets that inspires trust and sophisticated financial and industrial interrelationships is not present in Asia. Economic ties in this region have a fragility unlike the situation in Western Europe.

Moreover, the end of the cold war reduced security tensions in Asia much less than it did in Europe. On the Korean peninsula, North Korea remains a closed and unpredictable society. On the mainland, China persists as the last bastion of Communist ideology and institutions. Its economic reforms do not guarantee political openness and may only generate formidable new economic competition for Japan and the United States in bilateral, regional, and global markets. A leadership struggle after Deng and the scheduled transfer of Hong Kong in 1997 put the fate of Hong Kong, southern China, and perhaps also Taiwan, the most dynamic region in Asia, in a precarious political balance. Russia's military threat and presence in Asia have receded, but paradoxically Russia's weakness makes it less able to compromise on critical psychological issues, such as the return of the Northern Kurile Islands, which the USSR seized from Japan in the waning days of World War II.

How would Japan cope with a nuclearized North Korea or a resurgent or disintegrating Chinese state in the aftermath of a succession struggle? How does it lead a regionalized political community when it has so little political credibility, either in terms of its recognition of past moral responsibilities for war or the openness of its own society and policy processes for influence by neighboring countries? The only way it could do so again would be on the basis of sheer power. Japan's economic weight is growing in Asian countries.[13] There has been some modest regionalization of trade in Asia. But the degree of internal integration has not yet returned to prewar levels and is still well below that in Western Europe.[14] Japan's military power is already formidable. Japan has the second largest defense budget in the world after the United States. Although the defense share of GDP is much smaller, the size and potential use of Japanese military power are much feared by Asian countries as well as by many citizens in Japan itself. Japan shares a Confucian culture with China and other Asian states and may be able, on this basis, to negotiate Machiavellian-type pacts to carve up markets and influence inside and outside the region. If this type of political and security community should emerge in Asia, however, it will not be compatible with U.S. and Western political ideals and security interests. Such a regional bloc will inevitably be more closed and aggressive toward American and other outside interests.

Some analysts, in describing a significantly different Japanese model for security, politics, and economics, seem to welcome it. They see a Japan-centered Asian model of politics and economic development as not only politically incompatible with the West but also economically more successful.[15] If they are right, America has far bigger problems in Japan and Asia than trade in semiconductors or cellular telephones. A Japanese- or Chinese-led growth community in Asia will not be politically stable, except by force of arms, and will either expand aggressively into political and economic adventures in other parts of the world or degenerate into a highly conflictual and less prosperous region. Japan and China will coexist warily and create high levels of bilateral and regional tension. One wonders why strategic trade analysts, who are so unhappy with Japanese trade policies, are at the same time so sanguine about the prospects for Japanese geopolitical leadership.

A Trade and Security Bloc of the Americas

Ironically, the most likely regional community to evolve in the future, in terms of the political and security prerequisites, is a United States-led North American and Western Hemispheric community. The end of the cold war has removed the primary security tension in this region, namely Communist insurrection (with the exception of Cuba, which is nevertheless clearly on the defensive), and the United States faces no potential political rival in the region, unlike the potential rivalry between Russia and the EU in Europe or Japan and China in Asia. There will remain, of course, sources of internal instability, particularly poverty, corruption, and militarism, which are endemic in the hemisphere. U.S. power, however, is undoubtedly sufficient to address these instabilities. As a dominant power, the United States will also project a relatively open political and economic presence in the region, which will co-opt as well as coerce countries to pursue policies compatible with U.S. interests.

The issue is whether U.S. national interests can be confined to the Western Hemisphere alone. Can the United States "hide out" in the Western Hemisphere if tensions increase in Europe between the EU and a chaotic transition in the former Soviet empire or in Asia between Japan and China and their neighbors? The answer, after two world wars and a cold war, surely seems to be no. Even if it were yes, the question would arise as to what kind of society America might become at home, exercising its influence in the world largely as a regional, imperialist power in the Western Hemisphere. Clearly, U.S. growth would slow, as the poorer Western Hemispheric markets made meager substitutes for richer markets in Europe and Japan. U.S. social politics would also become more contentious, as increasing trade with poorer Latin American countries displaced American workers and potentially heightened animosities between Hispanic and other American groups. The NAFTA debate in 1993 showed that a good part of the country remains suspicious of economic integration with neighboring countries that have much lower wage rates, much higher political corruption, and much less respect for the environment. As NAFTA and hemispheric trade become more important than trade outside the hemisphere, pressures would grow to wall off these low-wage southern neighbors from American markets, jobs, and citizenship. And with fewer gains to be acquired through more lucrative economic ties with Europe and Japan (ties that in this scenario will be relatively declining), "American" jobs would be even scarcer and more contested than before.

This discussion of regional politics and trading blocs leaves one sad but inevitable omission—Africa. In whose bloc will Africa fall? Just asking the question answers it. Very likely, no one's. The EU has the closest ties with North and sub-Saharan Africa; the United States, with Egypt and the horn of Africa (most recently, in Somalia). In a more regionalized world, however, one might expect the EU to assume more responsibility, at least at the margins, for the horn of Africa as well as for the Middle East. But with its commitments in the former Soviet bloc, Europe will not have much energy or resources left over to devote to this area, even to the immediate Mediterranean zone. Moreover, if development of the former Communist Europe succeeds, Europe will have new, bountiful sources of energy and raw materials and become even less dependent on countries to its south and southeast. One wonders, given the reservations EU countries have regarding Muslim countries and their potential membership in the EU (for example, Turkey), whether Europe over time will pay much attention to this region at all, except as a source of potential disturbances and instability (the thrust of some recent concerns of European members in NATO about NATO's southern frontier with Islam).

The Democratic Industrial World—A Global Solution

This discussion of regional political communities and trading blocs suggests that the United States and its cold war industrial allies are less likely to be able to deal with their security and trading interests on a regional than on a global (that is, trilateral) basis. The global approach is more commensurate with overlapping security interests, both U.S. security interests in Europe and Asia and German and Japanese security interests in a U.S. security role in these regions. It is also more compatible with the economic costs. The industrial nations taken together constitute a historically unprecedented group of wealthy and democratic countries that can afford the future security and economic costs of transition in the former Communist world and the developing nations of Asia, Africa, and Latin America. Alone, or regionally, they cannot.

What is more, the democratic and advanced industrial world is not about to fall apart. One of the most reassuring developments of the post–cold war world is that, almost six years after the collapse of the Berlin Wall and the iron curtain in Europe, NATO, GATT (now WTO), and the EU are remarkably alive and well. If they are a bit frazzled, it is partly because so much continues to be expected of them. NATO steps up to new challenges in central Europe and Bosnia; the GATT concludes a new multilateral trade round and transforms itself into a stronger World Trade Organization; and the EU both completes a Maastricht Treaty, deepening European integration to include economic and monetary union as well as possible foreign policy and security cooperation, and simultaneously widens the union to include three new members in January 1995: Austria, Sweden, and Finland.

The mere presence of this democratic world of peaceful and free market–oriented countries exerts a substantial, albeit often silent, influence on the contemporary world. Does anyone believe that the Balkan conflict in the former Yugoslavia would not have blown up by now into a full-scale regional, if not global, war had industrial nations been competing with one another for military and political influence in this region as they were in 1914 at the outbreak of World War I? Or does anyone believe that the countercoup of reactionary forces in Russia in October 1993 would have failed so decisively had industrial nations been divided bitterly against one another as they were in the fall of 1917 when a similar countercoup in Russia by Bolshevik revolutionaries succeeded? Amid all the daily differences that emerge and persist among the industrial nations, particularly in the continuing crisis in the former Yugoslavia, it is easy to overlook the fundamental political and strategic unity of the industrial countries and the pacifying presence this unity exerts on contemporary international affairs. Let this presence erode progressively or disappear into a regionalized world of security and trading blocs, and the United States and its erstwhile allies will wake up in a world fraught with much greater dangers and potential human costs than the one in which they now live.

None of this means that regional trade blocs will or should not emerge. As the NAFTA and early birth pains of APEC suggest, they are already doing so. What it does mean is that if regional trade blocs are not going to work at cross-purposes with national security interests, in both the United States and allied countries, they must proceed alongside the continuing liberalization of global trade among regions. Regionalism is not incompatible with the GATT.[16] GATT only sets conditions for regionalism. Liberalization within regions must be extensive (reduction of tariffs to zero) to ensure that regional agreements do not become easy ways to discriminate against third parties. And regional communities must be more trade creating than trade diverting. The common external tariff established by the new region must not be, on the whole, higher or more restrictive than the duties and regulations applicable to preunion trade relations. Regionalism, in short, was not intended to be an alternative to global liberalization but, as Jagdish Bhagwati puts it, "a *supplemental,* practical route to the universal free trade that GATT favored as the ultimate goal."[17]

If global freer trade stalls, however, regionalism becomes divisive. In the absence of global rules, proliferating free trade areas become discriminatory and *preferential.* They begin to clutter up the global economy with a confusing array of regional trade rules, particularly rules of origin. These rules derive from the fact that members of a free trade area retain separate external tariffs and therefore have to put a trace on goods entering the free trade area to ensure that imports do not enter the tariff-free area through the member with the lowest external tariffs. Proliferating free trade areas also increase the temptation to shift costs of liberalization within these areas to countries outside the free trade area. Finally, they enhance the prospect that industrial countries such as the United States and Japan will have a dominant advantage in regional markets populated largely by smaller and poorer countries.[18] Ironically, the United States, by virtue of its balanced trade ties with all three major regions of the world (Europe, Asia, and Latin America), would be in the catbird's seat, "with favored access to most of the markets in Latin

America, East Asia and Europe, while no other country would enjoy anything like this status."[19]

The key, therefore, to preventing the fragmentation of global markets and the privileging of industrial powers in regional markets is what happens at the global level, particularly in trilateral relations among the three key industrial nation actors—the United States, the European Union, and Japan. Is expanding trade liberalization at the global level obsolete?

4

Alleged Obstacles
to Global Freer Trade

What are the obstacles to continued and deepened global trade cooperation among Europe, Japan, and the
United States? According to strategic trade analysts,
the obstacles are numerous and probably insurmountable.
The first obstacle they believe is political—the different
cultures, economies, and institutions of these countries.
The U.S. system is based on liberal Anglo-American values
of individual freedom and consumer economic choice.
The European system is based on more collectivist and
egalitarian standards emphasizing social as opposed to individual goals and involving a greater role for the state in
education, health, the economy, media, and environment.

The Japanese system, borrowed partly from Europe
(especially Germany), is racially homogeneous and oriented toward authoritarian and oligopolistic structures in
the government and economy that systematically discriminate against foreigners and the possibility of genuinely
open markets. These differences involve less government
intervention in trade and economic relations in the United
States, more in Europe, and most in Japan and preclude
the possibility of global trade relations based on common
rules and procedures as practiced by the GATT during

the cold war. To be fair, strategic trade advocates conclude, trade relations have to be reconstituted on the basis of outcomes, not rules. Governments have to support industries and exports directly and negotiate market shares bilaterally and regionally, using economic muscle to balance global competition among the trilateral democracies, much like military power balanced political competition between the United States and the Soviet Union in the cold war.

A second obstacle to global freer trade, according to strategic trade policy theologians, is a changed international marketplace. Trade competition is no longer a matter of *comparative* advantage among countries in terms of fixed resource endowments (labor, land, and natural resources) but *competitive* advantage in terms of mobile capital and technology resources.[1] Scale economies to develop advanced technology and finance modern production are so huge that only governments and oligopolistic corporations can play this game. Thus, individual national governments cannot afford to sit back and let laissez-faire competition drive markets under common rules; they must intervene directly and pervasively to restructure old industries and create new ones. They must fight for market share and wage economic warfare, not just because other industrial nations are doing so but because "objective" conditions in the marketplace require it.

Strategic trade theory vastly overstates the obstacles to continued freer trade at the global level. Rivalry among the major capitalist countries is not a serious obstacle to freer trade, particularly between Europe and the United States. And the only choice with Japan is to press ahead toward more open markets, because if Japan retreats to insular and imperialist policies, the United States has lost far more in Asia than markets. In addition, basic market conditions have changed far less than strategic trade theorists assert. The strategic trade argument is not really new; it is the infant industry argument of neoclassical economics writ large for the nation. And the infant industry argument did not *preclude* freer trade: it *presumed* freer trade.

Strategic trade theory also presumes freer trade. The Asian model of development celebrated by strategic trade theorists works only in the context of the Anglo-American model of freer trade. No one has shown that Japan or any other Asian country would have succeeded in its trade and economic strategies, whatever the degrees of government intervention, if it had not had access to world markets, particularly the American market. To attribute such success to a superior development model, to domestic industrial, technology, and trade policy intervention, therefore, is at best a half-truth. Without global freer trade, the intervention model either fails or leads, because of its massive inefficiencies, to imperialism. The experience of former Communist countries testifies to the first outcome, and the recent transformation of South Africa (which built a reasonably prosperous economy on the back of apartheid and the exploitation of neighboring countries) provides evidence for the second. Strategic trade policy, like the infant industry alternative, works for follower countries and firms, not for leaders. Leaders need the uncertainty of undirected competition to create new knowledge; followers need only the certainty of access to existing knowledge in the leaders' markets. The Japanese are on the verge of learning this general truth; Americans need to be reminded of it.

Rival Capitalisms

Rivalry among capitalist countries is not an obstacle to freer trade. Within limits, differences in endowments and economic cultures and institutions are what create efficient markets; they are not obstacles to such markets. The fact that Japan saves more and the United States consumes more and that therefore Japan runs large trade and current account surpluses and exports capital to the United

States and other countries is not an obstacle to growth. It is a source of growth. If Japan could not transfer its savings to other countries, it would be poorer because it could export less, and other countries would be poorer because they could import and invest less. Make no mistake about it, if the United States or Japan attempts to reduce these trade and capital imbalances by means other than increasing investment for domestic expansion in Japan or increasing savings in the United States, growth will suffer. Reducing savings in Japan and decreasing investments in the United States will only make both countries worse off. This is not a question of abstract economic identities: it is a fact borne out amply by the world's experience in the 1930s.

Different economic capacities and institutions, therefore, do not impede growth. Political differences, however, may. Political leaders and public opinion may object to trade and current account imbalances and the flow of savings across national boundaries, presumably because they fear that, while benefiting both countries, such flows may cause one country to grow faster than the other. If *relative* gains become more important than absolute ones, one country may accept lower growth as long as it maintains its position vis-à-vis the other country. This is the point that American public opinion may have reached in 1990, at least according to one poll, when a majority of Americans interviewed said they preferred lower economic growth if it meant that Japan would not gain relatively on the United States.[2] At the extreme, this reaction leads to serious political conflict and the termination of economic relations. One country becomes convinced that the other country will use faster growth to harm the national interests of the first country. That is why strategic trade theorists have an obligation to spell out the larger national interests over which they see Japan and the United States parting company. How exactly is Japan likely to use its faster growth to harm U.S. interests, and how might the United

States purchase some inexpensive insurance against these possibilities?

Any assessment today of such differences among the United States, Japan, and Europe would not seem to support an extreme reaction to close or manage markets. These countries are closer together today than they have ever been in the past. The issue is not whether Japan is as open a market and society as the United States or whether governments play a greater role in Europe than in the United States. The issue is where these countries stand today compared with where they have been in the past.

Europe today is a continent of free societies. With the postwar liberalization of Spain, Portugal, and Greece, Western Europe became completely free of fascist, nationalist regimes. Today, the rest of Europe from the Elbe to the borders of China is struggling to free itself of Communist, totalitarian regimes. We should not forget that this is the Europe of divided nations and power politics that plagued the American republic from its inception and dragged this country into two hot wars and one cold war in this century. That this part of the world is or is now becoming fully free and democratic is an unprecedented historical situation, one that towers over the continuing differences between European and American economic interests and institutions. To equate rival capitalisms among these countries to the rival nationalisms and ideological struggles of the past or to speak about economic warfare in this context is an unpardonable parody of history.

Of course, Europe could turn inward again or drift off toward another rendezvous with Romanticism and its eastern, authoritarian traditions. Some analysts worry that the end of Europe's division may revive Germany's "eastern" identity and ambitions and lead to a German-led grouping of *Mitteleuropa* that rejects liberal capitalism or significantly modifies it to shape a third way between capitalism and communism.[3] The likelihood of such a development, however, seems very small. At least, it is not natural or inevitable, as proponents suggest. It would in fact require a host of misfortunes and mistakes in policy not only in Germany but in the countries of East and central Europe, the former Soviet Union, the European Union, and the United States. It presumes a non-Western oriented development in Russia, a failure of democracy in the Baltic and former Warsaw Pact countries, a severe weakening of the European Union, and a dramatic diminution of U.S. influence in Europe.[4] All this might happen but not soon or with any certainty. Moreover, German policy is seeking to counter rather than encourage and exploit such developments. It has reaffirmed NATO as a means to retain American influence in Europe, it worries about the democratic deficit and a weakening of the European Union (as much as, if not more than, France, the traditional proponent of European institutions), it has moved cautiously in asserting its influence in former Soviet bloc countries, and it has clearly pinned its hopes on the success of liberal reformers in Russia.

A greater concern is that Germany may be reluctant or unwilling to accept the social consequences of being the central power of a democratic Europe. Even if democracy and markets succeed in the East, economic and social disparities will remain, and Germany will probably continue to be the bull's-eye of social interactions and criss-crossing immigration in Europe for some time to come. In the face of this, Germany retains a definition of citizenship that denies immigrants full rights to participate in its society unless they can prove they have some German blood. This requirement is a vestige of an old racist definition of nationhood. Most major countries in Europe do not have such a requirement.[5] And it is inconsistent with the prospect of German and European leadership in the future European Union. Nations lead as much by their internal standards and openness to influence as by their external exercise of power. Germany, after its own successful struggles against both fascism and communism, is a country that has much to offer other European countries that are now struggling to free themselves of authoritarian pasts. If the new Europe is to become the tolerant, open, multicultural society it promises to be (and across Europe, as opposed to inside any one country, the European Union is even more multiethnic and multicultural than America), the country in the center has to offer citizenship to immigrants who learn its language and commit themselves to its customs and laws, whether or not they have German blood. Immigration can always be controlled and must be (otherwise, unchecked immigration raises new requirements for Lebensraum), but the principles of openness and tolerance toward greater immigration will be critical to signal the real difference between the new Germany and the old, and the new Europe and the old.

Japan presents a tougher case. Is it sufficiently open and democratic to coexist with Europe and the United States on the basis of a common set of rules and procedures that obviate settling day-to-day trade and other issues through diplomatic negotiations? Again, the comparison to be made is not so much between Japanese democracy and American or European democracy but between Japan today and Japan before the war and between Japan today and other Asian countries. To compare Japanese democracy with European or American democracy is an exercise in abstract philosophy, not a pragmatic consideration of present-day realities. Of course, Japan is not as open as Western democracies. By almost any measure—mixture of population (99.5 percent homogeneous), foreign imports, investment by foreign multinationals, willingness to accept refugees, even numbers of foreign students and tourists—Japan is the least accessible industrial country. But Japan does not exist in a vacuum. Compared with almost any other country in *Asia*, Japan is more open and politically accountable. And it is more open and accountable than it was in 1945. The realistic point of reference is China, South Korea, Malaysia, and other Asian countries, because these are the countries with which the United States and Europe have to relate, with or without Japan. If Japan is judged to be too inaccessible to deal with on the basis of common civil and commercial rules and procedures, does this mean that all of Asia is excluded from a rules-based global trading system? Or, just as dubiously, does it mean that a rules-based system should be rejected altogether, even between Europe and America, because one country in Asia, judged in the abstract, fails to meet the standards of openness established by revisionist critics of Japanese democracy? The strategic trade policy and revisionist critics of Japan overlook one important fact: Japan is the only bridge for Western interests in the Pacific. It is a beachhead, albeit only a beachhead, of democracy in Asia. It is the only partner with whom the United States can defend its multiple interests in Asia—on the mainland of China and periphery countries, in the South China Sea and Indian Ocean, and, for that matter, throughout the Pacific Rim (since Australia and New Zealand are too far away to offer anything but a base for defensive operations, as the United States learned in World War II).

What is more, Japan is changing. Critics, convinced that Asian and American cultures are fundamentally incompatible, doubt it[6] but other observers and daily events appear to confirm it.[7]

Studies show that the aging of the Japanese population and the passing of the baby-boom bubble in the United States will reduce both savings propensities in Japan and consumption propensities in the United States.[8] In addition, the cost of capital in Japan is rising, reducing the excess investment and capacity that fueled Japanese exports.[9] Similarly, trade profiles are converging, as Japan's revealed comparative advantage shifts toward higher value-added, technology-intensive products. This development intensifies the "head-to-head" competition between U.S. and Japanese (and European) industries.[10] But it also means that Japan, like other industrial economies, is facing mounting pressures to move its economy into the information and service sectors, to transnationalize its corporate investments and alliances, and to stay up with or get ahead of its competitors by deregulating domestic markets and becoming more engaged in foreign markets.

Politically, change is also accelerating in Japan. In early 1994, Japan passed a political reform bill that completely redraws the legislative districts in Japan.[11] Sometime in the next year or so, elections will be held under the new system, which emphasizes single-member constituencies (and hence more direct party competition) and gives liberal urban, consumer-oriented voters more weight than conservative rural, agricultural- and production-oriented voters. Party alignments are in flux. The Liberal Democratic Party (LDP), which held office for thirty-eight years (1955–1993) has splintered, and although it held office in early 1995 in an unlikely coalition with the old Socialist Party, reform parties merged into a new, single party in late 1994, the New Frontier Party, to challenge LDP leadership. If the measure is American-style democracy, these changes still fall short. But if the measure is increasing the influence of Japanese citizens who want more foreign products and lower prices in their society and who prefer to save less and consume more, the reforms may be sufficient to keep the U.S. and Japanese economies and balance-of-payments relations within the limits of political tolerance of the citizens and leaders of both countries. That is all that is required to maintain and expand America's toehold in Asia. Asking for more is an abstraction and a pastime of revisionist theorists.

No fundamental political obstacle exists to maintaining and even expanding a rules-based trading system among the major industrial trading partners. Europe is clearly an acceptable rules-based partner, even by the standards of strategic trade policy analysts. A recent study by Robin Gaster and Clyde Prestowitz, both advocates of results-oriented trade relations, concludes:

> In the realm of economics, what unites America and the European Union is far more important than what has been driving them apart. As highly developed industrialized regions with fully democratic governments and relatively generous welfare states, the United States and the EU share common values and common problems.[12]

And Japan, if it does not measure up to this standard, is at least the most open and democratic partner that the United States and Europe have in East Asia. Perhaps, as the above study recommends, the United States and Europe should cooperate more to accelerate Japanese openness, rather than conclude that such openness will never be sufficient to maintain a rules-based system with Japan. This recommendation is a refreshing proposal, especially coming from acknowledged revisionists who usually argue that we should live with Japanese differences rather than try to change them. Many Japanese welcome such foreign pressure for change, sensing that this pressure is not foreign in the sense of coming from an adversary that threatens Japan's sovereignty but is pressure that actually supports many of the goals Japanese citizens have set for themselves.

Changing International Market Conditions

A second obstacle to global free trade, strategic trade advocates insist, is the changing nature of the international marketplace.[13] Trade opportunities are no longer determined by fixed land and labor endowments but by mobile capital and technological resources, by economies of scale, and by learning experiences. Comparative advantage, therefore, is not inherited, based on geography, climate, size of population, and the like; it is created, based on innovations, a continuously educated work force, and access to global financial resources. Moreover, countries today do not trade different products in complementary industries (for example, raw materials for manufactured goods); they trade products in the same industry (different producers of automobiles and automobile components, for instance) and increasingly compete head-to-head for the same markets.[14]

In such competition, some win and others lose (unlike complementary trade where everyone wins), and the prize goes to the quickest and the biggest. It goes to the quickest because, with the emphasis on innovation, advantage does not last very long. Firms must quickly apply innovations, establish production, and acquire market share at home and abroad. And success goes to the biggest because only the biggest firms have access to the capital resources worldwide that are needed to start production quickly and to benefit from the economies of scale and cross-sector externalities that characterize most new products. Scale economies mean that the larger the market share a firm has, the more it produces, and hence the lower its average costs become, the more it learns, and the better able it is to invent and innovate the next generation of products (such as semiconductors) and related equipment (the machines to make semiconductors). Once a firm is far enough along this learning curve, it is argued, the barriers to entry for competitor firms become insurmountable. New firms cannot enter the market because they face massive capital costs and technological hurdles. The markets are eventually dominated by a few firms that gain early entry. Thus, instead of being competitive, new world markets are increasingly oligopolistic. And oligopolistic markets create opportunities for exploitation. The "invisible hand" does not work in such markets because firms may collude to manipulate prices, first lowering them to drive other competitors out of the market and then raising them to exploit oligopolistic rents.

According to the new trade theology, governments are central players in this kind of competition. They help firms acquire the technology, capital, and market share that lead to dominance. In the old markets of complementary industries, governments merely create the background music (establishing property rights, antitrust practices, sound macroeconomic policy, and the like.) In competitive markets, they become stage directors, subsidizing research and development and loans to specific industries, protecting home markets to help firms build market share, and targeting foreign markets through predatory (that is, below-cost) pricing of exports.

None of these arguments is disputed in theory. Indeed, such arguments have been around for a long time. Strategic trade theory, the label given to the combination of arguments sketched above, is the old infant industry argument in neoclassical markets applied more generally to leading-edge, high-technology industries. The force of the arguments does not depend on theory but on whether they describe contemporary realities in world markets and whether they prescribe policies that can be shown by argument and experience to be better (that is, more beneficial to a particular country) than traditional freer trade policies.

On closer inspection, strategic trade arguments do *not* describe contemporary market realities very accurately. Nor do they prescribe policies that have a proven track record of success. Global market conditions today are probably less oligopolistic than they were ten, twenty, or thirty years ago. In the 1950s, U.S. firms dominated almost all manufacturing and high-tech markets. Today, most of these markets are contested, and new firms from industrializing countries (for example, Taiwan, Singapore, South Korea, Brazil, and Mexico) are entering these markets every year. What is more, strategic trade studies have not demonstrated which policies of government intervention work and which do not. The evidence they develop is based entirely on case studies, few of which examine failures of government intervention policies. Without evidence of policies that worked in one context and not in another, no conclusions can be drawn about which policies are in fact important or appropriate. Most damaging methodologically, all these case studies pull individual countries out of the context of global free trade in which domestic intervention policies are said to have worked. They ascribe success to domestic policies, when in fact access to open international markets may have been the overriding influence on policies, guiding interventionist strategies in directions consistent with market forces and greater efficiency.

Strategic trade theory became popular largely as an explanation of Japanese policies, but it describes quite well the earlier evolution of American policy in militarily strategic industries, such as aircraft, nuclear power, and electronics. The aircraft experience is particularly revealing. Through its defense programs, a "strategic" program in the old-fashioned sense of the term, the U.S. government "subsidized and boosted" the American commercial aircraft industry by encouraging new technology development and by providing large initial market orders for military aircraft, both at home and through exports to allied nations during the cold war.[15] The spin-off benefits of military aircraft for civilian purposes were substantial, and the U.S. aircraft industry dominated world commercial markets after World War II. Firms such as Boeing continue to do so today. While commercial spin-offs today may be less (the stealth bomber, for example, produces fewer commercial benefits than the B-52), those benefits were significant in the past and are probably still more substantial in present programs than American critics of Japanese policies like to admit (eager to show, as they are, that subsequent Japanese commercially directed "strategic" trade policies were far more egregious and reprehensible than earlier American defense technology policies).

U.S. government policy also played a key role in the early development of the merchant semiconductor industry[16] and the civilian nuclear power industry.[17] U.S. merchant (that is, nonintegrated) producers of semiconductors emerged in the late 1950s and 1960s, strongly supported by defense orders for solid-state rocketry and nuclear weapons production. Similarly, U.S. firms won the early *guerre des filieres* or battle of civilian nuclear power reactors in Europe and marketed U.S. light-water moderated reactors around the world, at least in part because the U.S. government had made a heavy front-end investment in these reactors as the propulsion mechanism for nuclear submarines.

Given this history of American oligopolists, or indeed monopolists, in early postwar markets, it is difficult to establish the empirical fact that markets today are more oligopolistic than they were before. If oligopolies constitute the "dominant form of supply structure in most R&D intensive or high technology industries" today, as studies suggest,[18] they almost certainly did so in key sectors such as aircraft, nuclear power and electronics right after the war. Indeed, oligopolistic markets, to the extent they exist today, are probably more welfare enhancing than they were before. Today they are less dominated by only one or two producers, and they involve competitors from several different countries. Airbus challenges Boeing and McDonnell Douglas; Japanese and now Korean semiconductor firms service low-end semiconductor markets; and French, Japanese, Korean, Brazilian, and other international companies supply civilian nuclear reactors and components.

Growing competition in contemporary high-tech markets suggests that barriers to entry may not be as formidable in these markets as strategic trade theory suggests.[19] Competition in "open" high-technology markets may have a rolling feature to it. The most advanced countries initially create these markets through higher levels of skill (research and development) and capital financing, while less advanced but newly industrializing countries eventually break into these markets, albeit at a substantial cost. If this is the case, it raises the interesting question whether initially dominant firms ever remain dominant long enough to recoup costs and exploit oligopolistic rents.[20] Strategic trade theory argues that losses from predatory pricing at the beginning to build up market share are made up through oligopolistic rents after competitors have been driven from the market. But judging from the profit picture of semiconductor producers in Japan today, it is not clear that firms remain dominant for that long. Korean firms now challenge Japanese firms, and U.S. firms have made a comeback. Nor is it clear that firms make up for such losses through cross-subsidization, that is, gains made in downstream or related sectors—for example, computers—which benefit from the technological spillover of upstream activities, as in the semiconductor industry. American computer industries continue to outcompete Japanese firms worldwide and are now challenging their competitors in Japanese markets as well.[21]

Why then the sudden, spirited enthusiasm in some quarters for U.S. strategic trade policies? One reason may be that the decline and shift of U.S. defense spending toward less commercially applicable technologies have left the U.S. government without its primary, perhaps only, instrument for competing with other governments in strategic high-technology trade. The U.S. government feels stripped of a critical policy instrument for promoting technological advance when its firms are no longer the only oligopolists. Moreover, for the United States, it is particularly difficult to convert from a defense-oriented Advanced Research Projects Agency (ARPA) to a civilian-oriented one. The administration has less discretion and control vis-à-vis Congress in commercial as opposed to traditionally classified defense sectors. U.S. high-technology policy is more likely to wind up as pork-barrel politics.[22] This fact makes the Clinton administration's gamble on a vastly increased Advanced Technology Program in the Commerce Department particularly questionable. That program has been increased from $68 million in FY 1993 to $431 million in FY 1995 and a projected $744 million in FY 1997. It has little chance of achieving any continuity or coherence. A Republican-controlled Congress is determined to cut it, and commercial programs have fewer accounting mechanisms such as the requirement for performance of U.S. weapons in war (the Persian Gulf, for instance) to ensure that it produces tangible returns.

A second and more important reason for the exaggerated interest in strategic trade policy is that some analysts have overstated the accomplishments of the Japanese or Asian model of development. The success of this model is due at least as much to the existence of open, competitive *international* markets as it is to the guidance of *domestic interventionist* policies. Indeed, interventionist policies alone without access to open markets would have certainly failed in Asian countries, as they did in closed Communist countries and in Latin America or other developing nations that pursued import substitution policies.

The Asian Development Model

What is the evidence that strategic trade policies work? The available evidence is no more than anecdotal.[23] Based on case studies, it is also suspect methodologically. Case studies of individual countries inevitably abstract from the generalized international context. They emphasize particular rather than universal conditions and are accordingly prone to attribute causes of growth to policies within the country rather than to conditions in the general international environment. Hence, they make it appear that specific strategic trade or industrial policies are generating results that may actually be produced by more general or universal conditions, such as competitive pressures of open, international markets. Government policies are in fact no more than intervening, rather than causal, variables. Moreover, case studies cannot tell us what the specific benefits of any given policy may be unless case studies of success, in which a particular policy is present, are compared with case studies of failure, in which that policy is not present (and all other factors are assumed to be the same). Strategic trade policy studies have studiously avoided cases in which strategic policy explicitly fails. In the absence of such comparisons, case studies tell us nothing at all about what policies work or do not work.

The assumption behind strategic trade theory is that firms gain advantage through learning by doing. But the point is not just *that* they learn but *what* they learn and whether learning is intrinsic or depends on appropriate external circumstances.[24] After all, firms in the former Communist states exploited economies of scale and other factors to achieve dominant positions in their respective international (that is, Communist) markets. Apparently, however, they did not learn the right things, and they did not keep on learning new things as conditions changed.

One wonders, therefore, if East Asian NICs, beginning with Japan, succeeded with their strategic trade policies in the postwar period because they were onto a more sophisticated type of domestic economic and trade policy or because they were latecomers in global markets that were steadily and broadly liberalizing. In such markets, they were able to learn from others. They imported technology from more advanced countries, because in open markets technology is hard to protect (the opposite of what strategic trade theory argues when it assumes that barriers to entry are insurmountable). And they designed interventionist domestic strategies to produce and market this technology for global competition. As Pietro Nivola remarks, "The genius of Japanese industrial policy, at least in some sectors, lies in shielding the local market while encouraging firms to compete fiercely in international markets, *thereby maintaining efficiency*" (emphasis added).[25] This is classic infant industry behavior. Such policies do not create new markets, from which Japanese firms then extract and monopolize future rents; these policies challenge old or existing oligopolistic markets, already dominated by others, such as the United States, and divide up future rents in these markets more equitably. The question has always been how well these strategies work once the "infant countries" or latecomers such as Japan are no longer "late" but begin to operate more on the frontiers of new research and innovation.

All the evidence is not yet in, but the fact that the Japanese do not invent technologies as well as they apply them and that the United States has trouble capturing the benefits of new inventions for specifically U.S.-based companies suggests two things: (1) the Japanese are still behind the United States in moving into the information economy and will remain so until they broadly restructure their current manufacturing economy; and (2) American difficulties in capturing technology rents imply that markets at the frontier are more competitive than oligopolistic and that international strategic alliances with foreign firms may be a far better way to stay on the technological frontier than domestic strategic trade policies.

Despite all the hype about the Japanese and Asian development model, the plain fact is that Japan—and, for that matter, Germany as well—lags substantially behind the United States in the transition from a manufacturing-based to an information-based economy. Statistics compiled by the Organization for Economic Cooperation and Development show that the United States is far ahead of both Japan and Germany in moving employment and capital into the information and service sectors.[26] In 1990, 70.9 percent of the civilian work force in the United States was employed in services, compared with 56.8 percent and 58.7 percent respectively for Japan and Germany. As data in chapter 6 of this volume show, this shift of U.S. employment into the services has not come at the expense of manufacturing competitiveness or the manufacturing base of the economy. In recent years, America has experienced more rapid productivity growth in both manufacturing and services than either Japan or Germany (see table 6–1 in this volume). The transition, in fact, has been necessary to renew the manufacturing base of the U.S. economy. It is similar to the transition seventy-five years ago from an agriculture-based society to a manufacturing one. Agriculture was not "hollowed out" by the earlier transition, and manufacturing has not been hollowed out by the current one. Interestingly, the shrill alarms about hollowing out are now no longer heard in the United States but are increasingly heard in Japan. Firms in that country are facing the same requirement today that American firms faced much earlier to downsize employment in manufacturing and shift home-based manufacturing activities to offshore and outsourcing installations.[27]

The economic situation in Japan is in many respects appalling. A comparable situation in the United States has not existed since the late 1970s and early 1980s. Japan's economy has been flat for three years. The manufacturing sector is bloated and declining. Production has fallen 5.5 percent since 1990;[28] productivity in 1992 and 1993 (the last year for which data are available) was negative (see table 6–1 in this volume); surplus capacity exceeds 30 percent;[29] unemployment, both official and disguised, is estimated at 9 percent or more; and corporate profits recovered modestly in 1994 for the first time in five years.[30] The service sector is primitive. Japan is far behind the United States in installing desktop computers, local area networks, software and switching equipment, and similar information-oriented technologies. The retail, airline, telecommunications, and financial service sectors are only beginning the process of deregulation and restructuring that American companies undertook in the mid-1980s.[31]

The financial sector is a disaster. In June 1995, the Ministry of Finance disclosed for the first time official estimates of bad debts in the Japanese banking system. Problem loans on which principal payment has ceased or interest payments had been lowered or delayed totaled $475 billion. Unofficial estimates put this total at over $1 trillion.[32] The U.S. savings and loan crisis, in which some $200–300 billion were at stake, pales by comparison. Land prices in Japan have dropped by 50 percent, the stock market is down 60 percent, and Japanese investments overseas, especially in the United States, where only a few years ago the Japanese were portrayed as buying up America's trophies (such as Rockefeller Center, MCA, and Columbia Pictures,), have been selling off at 40–50 percent losses.[33]

No one should shed any tears for Japan. It is still a powerhouse economy and formidable economic competitor. But the hysteria over Japan Inc. was and is just that—hysteria.[34] Japan is a normal economy facing the same transition from a manufacturing-based to a service economy that America faced over a decade ago.

Why is Japan a decade behind if the Asian development model is so much better? Strategic trade theory has it all wrong. Japan did not succeed because it had a better model and became a leading-edge producer; it succeeded because it was and remains a follower, at least in the cutting-edge technologies of the information age. McKinsey and Company, an international management consulting firm, studied the sources of productivity leadership in specific industries around the world. It concluded that the most important factor in industrial success is "the intensity of competition to which managers are exposed and, more specifically, the degree to which they are faced by direct competition from producers on the leading edge."[35] Japan and the Asian NICs were not leading-edge producers for most of the postwar period and in many areas are still not today. It is hard to conclude therefore that they succeeded in the 1960s and 1970s primarily because they exploited superior domestic policies and competition and merely used global markets to dump their products on foreign consumers. A more plausible explanation is that their access to foreign markets and leading-edge producers in those markets exposed domestic companies to direct competition. This direct competition, in turn, provided the appropriate market-oriented signals to guide domestic interventionist strategies. In this explanation, causation runs not from domestic strategic policies to competitiveness to export success, but from international market competition to appropriate market signals to successful domestic interventionist strategies. Strategic trade theory, by abstracting individual country policies from the global marketplace, attributes success to domestic interventionist policies that properly belongs to international opportunities for the acquisition of technology in open, competitive world markets.

By getting the explanation wrong, strategic trade arguments give poor policy advice for today's markets. Because no one country dominates all important leading-edge technologies, success depends much more on strategic access to foreign markets and competition than on strategic protection of and intervention in domestic markets. Without foreign competition, the EC might never have been spurred to challenge the U.S. aircraft monopoly, U.S. automobile producers might never have restructured to challenge Tokyo imports, and Japanese electronic industries might never have rediscovered the need for profits, as they are doing today. Many Japanese firms have reached the limits of market-share strategies and found that because of new competition they have no opportunity to capture rents and recoup losses from earlier predatory pricing.

Still, it is possible, if not all countries pursue strategic trade policies and international markets remain relatively open and competitive, that some economic and trade policies may be of more benefit to a nation than freer trade policies. What is the evidence for this possibility? Once strategic trade policies are analyzed in the context of open and competitive international markets, rather than abstracted from them, it becomes difficult to distinguish those policies from traditional policies based on comparative advantage. Robert Wade, who is sympathetic to strategic trade theories, finds it difficult to know what the Koreans did, exactly, to achieve higher growth or whether they departed at all in what they did from what was prescribed by traditional comparative advantage theory. He finds, for example, that Korean "exports have been far more labor-intensive than overall production, a prediction in line with CA [comparative advantage] theory."[36] And although "it is also true that from the early 1960s, capital intensive industries producing intermediates have experienced rates of growth much higher than the manufacturing average, a phenomenon less readily reconciled with CA theory," this result, he notes, may be due not to capital intensity but to a highly skilled labor force (as a percentage of basically skilled or unskilled workers).

Korea invested in education, particularly higher education, that anticipated the skills that would be needed in the future marketplace. "So one hypothesis," he concludes, is that "Korea's industrialization . . . did not depart from CA to any significant extent." What Korea may have done is to "stretch" but not "create" the membrane of comparative advantage. Moreover, exactly how it did this remains a mystery, "because in many other countries efforts to stretch the CA membrane by investing in advance of skills so as to generate learning-by-doing effects have proved so costly that the projects have eventually folded."[37] Wade reaches similar conclusions for other East Asian countries,[38] and international comparisons between Latin American and Asian countries show that, while governments do play a role in all trade and development policy choices, "it is not clear that governments are free of traditional factors of comparative advantage in making their choices."[39]

More recent studies debunk the miracle of East Asian growth altogether. The growth model, it appears, was quite conventional. As in the case of the Soviet Union in the 1950s, it relied heavily on large inputs of labor and capital and did not achieve much by way of greater efficiency or productivity. As Paul Krugman writes, "If Asian success reflects the benefits of strategic trade and industrial policies, those benefits would surely be manifested in an unusual and impressive rate of growth in the efficiency of the economy." But, he notes, "There is no sign of such exceptional efficiency growth." "If there is a secret to Asian growth," he concludes, "it is simply deferred gratification, the willingness to sacrifice current satisfaction for future gain."[40] Asian citizens gave up current consumption in favor of savings, and these savings poured into massive capital investments both at home and abroad. Those investments were not always successful. The financial collapse in Japan over the past four years turned up massive inefficiencies, and Japanese investments, including those in the United States, produced disastrous losses, not profits.[41] Japan clearly overinvested in the manufacturing sector, particularly exports, and is now struggling to downsize an industrial sector outmoded by the information age. Even today, Japan invests twice the share of GDP that the United States does to achieve about the same or only a slightly higher rate of growth. Japanese capital investment is not the economic juggernaut that strategic trade theories make it out to be.

The U.S.-Japan Semiconductor Agreement

Wade's assessment of East Asian policies is attentive to the need to consider failures of interventionist policies as well as successes. By contrast, efforts to evaluate U.S. attempts at strategic trade policy seem determined to find success even in partial failures. Assessments of the U.S.-Japan Semiconductor Trade Agreement (STA), for example, reflect particularly tortured efforts to extract some small evidence of return from the agreement, even while conceding that aspects of the agreement definitely failed. Bergsten and Noland conclude, along with most analysts, that the anti-dumping provisions of the semiconductor agreement were a dismal failure, doing little more than turning U.S. markets into high-cost platforms for downstream production of products that use semiconductors (such as computers) and transferring large rents in the form of higher export prices to Japanese semiconductor producers.[42] But they find the market access provisions of the agreement, the securing of a 20 percent share for foreign semiconductor producers in Japanese markets, to be more arguably a success. After a daisy chain of Rube Goldberg–like assumptions, they conclude that foreign sales and exports were higher as a result of the agreement, but they note that technological innovations might have caused this increase rather than the agreement. Moreover, they acknowledge that even if all the assumptions behind this conclusion are correct, the market access agreement was not necessarily the best way to achieve the result. Alternatives might have been to subsidize the U.S. industry and then negotiate a bilateral and multilateral code of acceptable subsidies in the GATT (as the United States and the EU have done in agriculture), to negotiate access for U.S. firms to Japanese R&D consortia in return for the access of Japanese companies to U.S. consortia, or to reduce the cost of capital to U.S. firms by reducing the budget deficit.

Laura Tyson's assessment of the semiconductor agreement is still more favorable. Even in the case of the anti-dumping provision, she argues that higher prices helped new competitors enter the market, such as the Koreans, Taiwanese, and Europeans (Siemens, for instance). Moreover, according to her, the agreement did not cause higher prices. The Japanese cartel went into action to raise prices before the agreement.[43] The agreement then encouraged non-Japanese firms to reenter the market and to reverse Japanese gains in dynamic random access memories (DRAMs) and halt their gains in erasable programmable chips (EPROMs). Tyson also believes the agreement contributed to greater market access in Japan, the 20 percent market share arrangement. The Japanese met this commitment at the eleventh hour in late 1992. The market share then dipped as low as 18 percent in 1993, rising again above 20 percent in 1994. It is all but impossible to know whether the agreement or the market is responsible for these results.

In any case, the evidence that the semiconductor agreement was a success is rather meager. As Bergsten and Noland point out, the surge in foreign semiconductor sales in Japan can be attributed to "a plethora of tie ups involving U.S. and Japanese firms," and "it is difficult to say . . . how many of these were due to the STA and how many would have occurred anyway in response to business conditions."[44] Even Tyson notes that some important tie-ups, such as Motorola's alliance with Toshiba, were in the works before the semiconductor agreement was concluded.[45] Whatever the truth, there is no way to know it.[46] Case studies permit no generalizations or cause-effect conclusions, particularly when no effort is made to investigate cases that include failures as well as successes.

Interestingly, all strategic trade policy analysts agree that there are better ways to accomplish market opening than the use of market share arrangements (so-called voluntary import expansions). Tyson prefers countervailing subsidies but says this option was a nonstarter in the ideological environment of 1986.[47] Others, such as Bergsten and Noland, point out that encouraging transnational R&D consortia, that is, the kinds of alliances and tie-ups that helped to increase foreign chip sales in Japan, or reducing the budget deficit would accomplish the same thing. The key for U.S. government policy is to focus on and correct the things that are known to be distortions.

The U.S. budget deficit is clearly a distortion. At this stage, it is not known whether the Japanese form of industrial organization, the *keiretsu,* is a distortion or simply a more efficient mechanism for production.[48] If analysts dealt with known distortions in U.S.-Japan trade relations, especially at the macroeconomic level, they might go through fewer contortions to find sectoral distortions and then seek remedies through highly specific, and mostly marginal, bilateral trade agreements.

5

Trade and Domestic Economic Policies

The error of strategic trade policy theory is not to emphasize the link between international trade and domestic economic policy, for trade and domestic policies are fundamentally related. The error is to get the causal direction wrong, failing to recognize that international trade competition is the only reliable guide to efficient domestic market intervention. Another error is to overplay the role of domestic *microeconomic* policies when domestic *macroeconomic* policies are way out of line. Just as it is impossible to imagine the success of Japan and the Asian NICs without open markets, it is also impossible to imagine their success without sensible fiscal and monetary policies. U.S. macroeconomic policies, by contrast, have been much less satisfactory. Strategic trade policy advocates blame freer trade for what are essentially macroeconomic policy deficiencies.[1] Freer trade is not obsolete. What has become obsolete, unfortunately, is the common-sense recognition that trade competitiveness depends fundamentally on long-term price stability and medium-term market flexibility. Chronic budget deficits eventually undermine prospects for long-term price stability, and sectoral interventions to protect or subsidize individual industries or firms ultimately make labor and capital markets more rigid and less able to respond to competitive stimuli from open international markets.

Almost no economist and certainly no businessperson disagrees with the basic proposition that the mutual benefits of freer trade can be captured only if domestic (and corresponding exchange rate or international) prices remain *relatively* stable and domestic factor markets *relatively* flexible. Without stable prices, trade and investment, especially over the longer term, are subject to distortions and inefficiencies. Products and investments are made that cater to the short term. No one can reasonably predict what prices are likely to be over the lifetime of an investment (seven to twelve years) and therefore what the returns on that investment might be. Hence they do not invest in projects that go out beyond two to three years. Similarly, trade and investment activities will be stillborn or rigged if entrepreneurs cannot bid in open markets for the capital and labor they need and instead have to lobby government regulatory agencies or state-run financing programs to secure the necessary resources. Macroeconomic policies (monetary and fiscal policies) have the most important effects on price stability, and microeconomic or regulatory policies have most to do with enhancing or distorting the flexibility of domestic labor and capital markets.

Embedded Liberalism

The relationship between mutually beneficial freer trade and noninflationary domestic economic policies has been obscured by two misleading arguments in the postwar period. One is that the United States and Europe agreed after World War II to pursue *laissez-faire* policies in international markets on condition that they were free to pursue *interventionist* policies in domestic markets.[2] According to this thesis, external free trade was "embedded" in internal social commitments: free, commercial competition abroad was to be offset by social protection at home. Management gained access to foreign markets, while labor was assured of employment and rising incomes at home.

This argument misinterprets the agreements that established the postwar Bretton Woods system and the free trade regime of the GATT. These agreements did not sanction unlimited government intervention at home. The International Trade Organization (ITO), of which GATT was originally a part, did not come into being because the United States and other industrial nations objected to extensive provisions in the ITO for full employment and other policies to protect workers. What industrial nations, including the United States, did accept was a new role for government in the management of countercyclical macroeconomic policy. Governments committed themselves to run budget deficits in times of economic slowdown and budget surpluses in times of economic growth. They did not agree to pursue full employment policies, whatever the consequences for government budgets. Nor did they agree to extensive microeconomic interventions to allocate directly labor and capital resources in domestic markets.[3]

The data in figure 5–1 and figure 5–2 show the limits that prevailed on government interventions in the 1950s and 1960s. On average, over this period, budget deficits were low (0.2 percent of GDP in the United States, 0.7 percent of GDP in the other major industrial countries), reflecting cyclical Keynesian deficits (and surpluses), not the structural or chronic Keynesian deficits that came to characterize the policies of the United States and other major industrial nations in the 1970s and 1980s. Monetary policies were also restrained, especially in the United States, which provided the international reserve currency. Monetary policies in the other major industrial countries were more expansionary, creating higher inflation in these countries than in the United States (from 1947 to 1967, 4.4

FIGURE 5–1
Economic Policy and Performance Indicators for the United States, 1947–1992

Average annual % of GDP

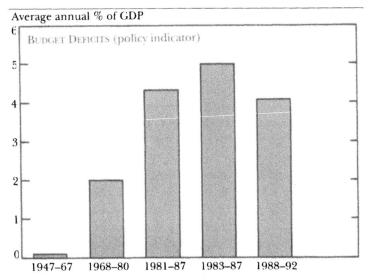

Average annual % change of M1 and M2

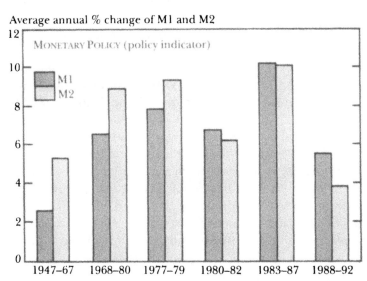

(Figure continues)

FIGURE 5-1 (continued)

Average percentage point change per decade
of government expenditures, as % of GDP

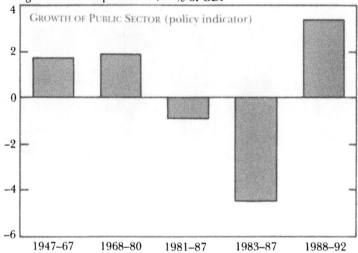

Average annual % change

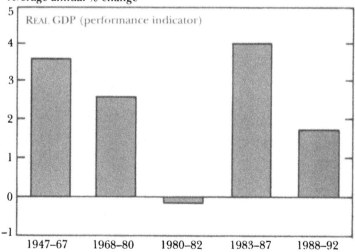

(Figure continues)

FIGURE 5–1 (continued)

Average annual % change in GDP deflator

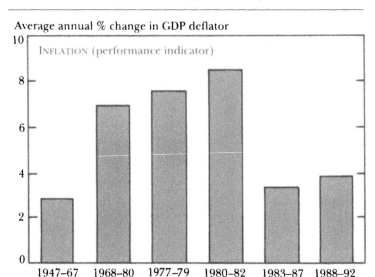

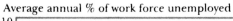

Average annual % of work force unemployed

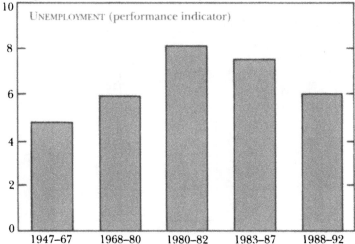

SOURCE: Adapted from Henry R. Nau, *The Myth of America's Decline: Leading the World Economy into the 1990s* (New York: Oxford University Press, 1990).

FIGURE 5–2
ECONOMIC POLICY AND PERFORMANCE INDICATORS FOR FRANCE,
GERMANY, JAPAN, AND THE UNITED KINGDOM, 1947–1992

Average annual % of GDP

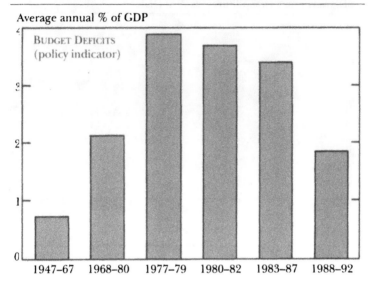

Average annual % change of M1 and M2

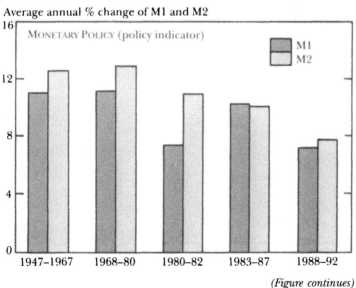

(Figure continues)

FIGURE 5–2 (continued)

Average percentage point change per decade
of government expenditures, as % of GDP

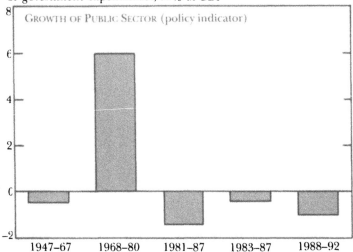

GROWTH OF PUBLIC SECTOR (policy indicator)

1947–67 1968–80 1981–87 1983–87 1988–92

Average annual % change

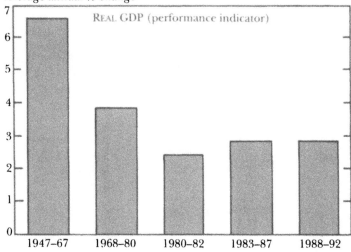

REAL GDP (performance indicator)

1947–67 1968–80 1980–82 1983–87 1988–92

(Figure continues)

FIGURE 5–2 (continued)

Average annual % change in GDP deflator

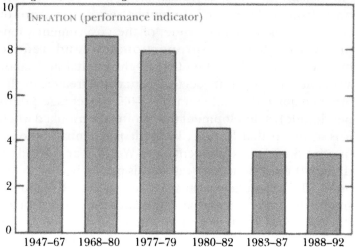

Average annual % of work force unemployed

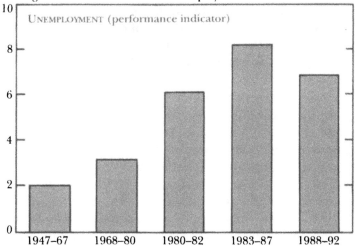

SOURCE: See source for figure 5–1.

percent per year versus 2.9 percent per year, respectively). In addition, the industrial nations in this period did not, relatively speaking, pursue more interventionist microeconomic (that is, industrial) policies. On the contrary, from 1947 to 1967 the public sector as a share of GDP (a measure, albeit crude, of the government's tendency to expand disproportionately and reduce microeconomic flexibility, that is, the capital and labor available to the private sector) actually retreated in the other major industrial countries (-0.5 percentage points per decade), a development that is often overlooked when it is assumed that Europe, in particular, embarked on a massive Socialist experiment after World War II. And although the public sector grew in this period in the United States (1.6 percentage points per decade), it did so from a smaller base and less so than it did after the 1960s. During the 1950s and 1960s, therefore, the basic domestic policy prerequisites were in place to make freer trade mutually beneficial, and preferences for freer trade policy reigned throughout the industrial world.

Domestic policies shifted sharply, however, in the 1970s and 1980s. This shift undermined the support for freer trade and initiated a process of creeping protectionism. Although the industrial nations clung to freer trade policies with one hand, they let go of the supporting, noninflationary domestic policies with the other. Budget deficits ballooned and remained high right on through the 1980s and the early 1990s. Monetary policies accommodated this fiscal expansion. Inflation undermined both domestic price stability and the fixed system of international exchange rates (which represent international prices). Meanwhile, as macroeconomic policy inflicted massive adjustment pressures on the microeconomy, microeconomic policy intervention accelerated and made capital and labor markets more rigid. The public sector exploded in the other major industrial countries in the 1970s, growing by 6 percentage points per decade. It also accelerated in the United States (1.9 percentage points per decade).

In the 1980s, macroeconomic policies in the major industrial nations improved in the monetary area but remained askew in the fiscal area. Monetary policies contracted to curb inflation (especially M1; see bar graphs in figure 5–1 for U.S. and figure 5–2 for other major industrial countries' monetary policies in the period 1980–1982), but fiscal deficits soared in the United States (to a record average of 5.0 percent of GDP 1983–1987) and remained high in the other major industrial countries (3.4 percent of GDP during the same period). The combination of tight money and loose spending in the United States created the high interest rates and high dollar of the early Reagan years. The high dollar, in turn, crippled trading interests in the United States, impeding exports and accelerating imports. Support for a new trade round languished. Eventually, monetary policy loosened again in the mid-1980s (see bar graphs in figure 5–1 and figure 5–2). The dollar tumbled, and enough support for freer trade revived to launch the Uruguay Round.

Despite the volatility of macroeconomic policy, substantial improvements were made in the 1980s in regulatory and microeconomic policies. Deregulation and privatization came into vogue, initially in Great Britain and the United States and then throughout the industrial and developing world. The public sector retreated dramatically in both the United States and other industrial countries, although rising again in the United States after 1988 (see bar graph in figure 5–1). Industrial productivity advanced smartly (see data in next chapter of this volume). American industry downsized and restructured to face international competition. Employment shifted rapidly into the service sectors. The United States made the move into the information age a full decade ahead of its industrial country competitors.

The failure to correct fiscal policies, however, exacted

its toll. After 1988, the most significant policy change in the United States and the other major industrial countries was once again toward tighter money (see last bar of monetary policy graphs of figure 5–1 and figure 5–2). Given persistent large budget deficits (which accelerated again in Germany after 1990), tighter money preserved gains in inflation, which remained low, but constrained domestic growth and intensified competition for export markets. Government intervention accelerated in the United States at a higher rate than ever before (3.5 percentage points per decade).

Given the breakdown and volatility of domestic policies over the past two and a half decades, it is little wonder that freer trade has produced fewer mutual benefits for industrial nations. The burden of debt from hemorrhaging budget deficits and accompanying private borrowing (consumer and corporate) slowed recovery in the United States in the early 1990s and now slows recovery in Europe and Japan. It was not freer trade policies that produced these results, however, but the collapse of supporting domestic policies that left free trade policy "out to dry" in an increasingly hostile and unstable macroeconomic environment.

The embedded liberalism argument obscures all these policy changes since 1945 and assumes that the excessive Keynesian policies of chronic budget deficits and expansionary monetary policies in the 1970s were merely continuations of the postwar compromise to offset freer trade competition with less free domestic capital and labor markets. In fact, of course, the postwar compromise of embedded liberalism, if it ever existed (which the above data put in doubt), was a "contradiction waiting to happen." At some point, pump priming of fiscal and monetary policies to achieve full employment and sectoral interventions to protect labor and allocate capital were bound to come into conflict with the requirements of freer trade. Pump priming and intervention produce unstable prices and exchange rates and less flexible labor and capital markets. These conditions, in turn, make it more difficult to meet the competition from imports and export markets. Industries cannot shift resources into more competitive activities and thus call for more favoritism and protectionism. Eventually, countries adopt strategic trade policies and managed sectoral trade agreements. The conflict between freer trade and new intervention policies becomes more intense precisely as freer trade succeeds in reducing the level of quotas and tariffs that would otherwise buffer the trade effects of domestic interventionist policies. Liberalization removes the border measures that insulate domestic economies from one another.[4] Inflation in one country now distorts markets in others, and intraborder domestic policies, such as subsidies and regulatory policies, become topics of bitter trade disputes. These disputes demonstrate emphatically that certain types of domestic interventions, particularly sectoral interventions, are not compatible with, but set sharp limits on, the potential for freer trade.

Embedded liberalism, if it intended to describe postwar trade policy, was not a compromise: it was a contradiction. The data suggest that it was never a very accurate description of what government policies actually were in the postwar period.

Export or Trade Pessimism

The second argument that distorted the relationship between freer trade and specific market-supporting domestic economic policies in the postwar period was the general view in developmental studies that freer trade was seldom appropriate or advantageous for poorer countries. Freer trade experiments generally failed in Latin America, it was pointed out, while interventionist, not freer, trade policies succeeded in Asia. The reason, it was argued, is that developing countries are generally poor and poor countries have a comparative advantage only in raw materials and products requiring low skills. These products face declining demand in world markets. Hence, freer trade, according to this logic, leads to adverse terms of trade. Developing countries receive less and less for their exports and pay more and more for their imports. Latin American countries that experimented with freer trade thus found no escape from the cycle of poverty. Asian countries that managed trade did find an escape. The solution to development problems accordingly was to do what the Asian developing countries did—spurn freer trade in favor of strategic industrial and technology policy interventions.

Often overlooked in this comparison, however, are broader domestic macroeconomic and structural policies. Asian NICs pursued exemplary domestic macroeconomic policies and designed interventions to address the market signals provided by highly competitive export markets abroad. They also invested heavily in education and health to create an efficient work force. Latin American countries, for the most part, completely mismanaged macroeconomic policies, protected inefficient industries from international competition, usually across the board, and neglected the education and health of their human resources.

Today, developing countries in Latin America and elsewhere around the globe have rediscovered the importance of sound domestic policies. They are bringing fiscal deficits and debt under control, making their monetary policies and institutions more independent of political control, privatizing industries and public services, and investing more in market-oriented infrastructure and human resources. As they have rediscovered the domestic policies that support and make freer trade policy more advantageous, developing countries, particularly in Latin America, are abandoning import substitution policies and seeking to join regional and global freer trade arrangements. The regional trade summits in late 1994 in both

Asia (APEC meeting in Indonesia in November) and Latin America (Miami summit in December) set dates (2020 and 2005, respectively) to implement freer trade agreements in these regions.

Unfortunately, as developing countries have finally come around to adopting the domestic and trade policies the United States and other industrial countries have always advocated for them, the industrial countries have become more reluctant to include low-wage developing countries in freer trade arrangements. Strategic trade policy advocates in industrial countries now preach a new theology of national economic security to protect jobs from the low-wage competition and lax environmental standards in developing countries. That developing countries have a natural comparative advantage in low-wage industries and, being poor, might be expected, at least in comparison with industrial nations, to place more emphasis on growth than environment seems to escape or at least not concern the new strategic trade theologians.

Thus, the leading arguments of the postwar period that dealt with the links between domestic and trade policies, embedded liberalism and export pessimism, obscured the dependence of freer trade policies on sound domestic fiscal, monetary, regulatory, and infrastructure (particularly for human resources) policies. Domestic policies had to maintain three basic conditions for freer trade to work—relatively stable prices (and exchange rates), relatively flexible labor and capital markets that could reallocate resources over time from less efficient sectors to more efficient ones, and a healthy and well-trained work force. Asian policies, generally speaking, established all three conditions. The embedded liberalism argument emphasized only the last condition: favorable wage and other conditions for workers. And import substitution policies in developing countries ignored all three conditions. Under these circumstances, freer trade policy was bound to languish among both industrial and developing countries.

The lowering of trade barriers that took place in the 1950s and 1960s ran head-on into the raising of interventionist barriers to create full employment and protect workers that took place in the 1970s and 1980s.

By this account, therefore, it was domestic policies that changed and weakened the benefits of freer trade, not conditions in international markets that made freer trade obsolete. Thus, if domestic policies change again, back to more stable prices and flexible factor markets, the mutual benefits of freer trade can be recaptured. The stage would be set for a vast revitalization and expansion of global freer trade arrangements. Such an expansion would be extremely timely, coming at the moment when former Communist countries and many developing nations are struggling to rid themselves of the closed markets and closed societies that enslaved their peoples for four decades or more. There are no significant obstacles to this expansion. The obstacles lie not in market conditions but in the way leaders think about trade, jobs, and national economic security.

The debate in the Clinton administration, therefore, is more critical than ever. Strategic trade policy advocates offer one view; traditional freer trade policy advocates another. The linchpin of this debate is how the two sides view America's capacity to compete. Strategic trade policy advocates disparage the strength of the American economy and export competitiveness, in part perhaps because they are still fighting the battles of the early and mid-1980s and are reluctant to concede the advances made in that decade. President Clinton's national security strategy statement of July 1994, for example, still talks about the need to "reverse the decline in American competitiveness that plagued our international economic performance for over a decade."[5] Freer trade policy advocates, in contrast, emphasize America's strengths but are, in some cases, prone to ignore the downside of domestic policies in the 1980s, particularly when they advocate further tax cuts without proportionate spending cuts. Deficits will eventually ruin the American economy as surely as protectionism will. Most likely, because they feed on one another, deficits and protectionism will combine to sink the American economy. Any sensible plan to seize the new opportunity for freer trade, therefore, has got to deal with both macroeconomic policy distortions and strategic trade policy protectionism.

6

America's Trade Competitiveness
Soars in the 1980s

If domestic economic policy distortions were corrected, new strategic trade policies would not be necessary. The evidence of the 1980s suggests as much. In that decade, American industry and the economy as a whole staged a major comeback, without the benefit of so-called strategic interventionist policies. An evaluation of this comeback has been badly misrepresented by political partisanship on both sides of the aisle. Examined with less passion, the evidence reveals that America's competitive position is far stronger than strategic trade policy advocates admit. This evidence further suggests, however, that American competitiveness has been held back by fiscal excesses. What if, in addition to the gains in inflation and total productivity that America achieved in the 1980s, the budget deficit had also been significantly reduced? Would we be debating the few tens of millions of dollars of additional sales from a relatively insignificant semiconductor agreement with Japan, or would we be enjoying a much improved current account balance and stronger recovery, burdened by less debt? The economic story of the 1980s in a nutshell is as follows:

- Total productivity in the United States rebounded

from a growth rate of 0.7 percent per year from 1973 to 1979 to a growth rate of 1.5 percent per year from 1980 to 1990.

• This growth was not enough to boost significantly the growth rate of real wages and living standards for American workers, which slowed to 0.7 percent annually after 1973. (Real wages did *not* decline, however; they just grew more slowly.)

• Paradoxically, because of this slowdown in average real wages, America was able to employ 40 million new entrants in the labor force after 1970, mostly women and minorities. (Lower wages encouraged companies to hire more workers.) Throughout the 1980s, the United States achieved and sustained much higher employment levels than Europe, where unemployment in the twelve EC countries soared from 3 percent to over 11 percent in the course of the decade. Even in comparison with its own past performance, U.S. unemployment went down during the decade, peaking in the recession in 1990 at only 7.3 percent compared with 10.8 percent in the recession in 1982.

• The growth in employment was concentrated in the service sector, into which the United States shifted much more rapidly than Europe or Japan.[1] Today, as noted in the previous chapter, Europe and Japan are just beginning to move employment into the information and service sectors.

• The shift into services did not reflect a hollowing out of the American manufacturing sector. The manufacturing sector accounted for the same share of GDP in 1990 as it did in 1950, around 23 percent. Net employment even increased in manufacturing. From 1979 to 1989, production workers in manufacturing fell 2.2 million, but nonproduction (that is, service) workers in manufacturing increased by 6.5 million, a net gain of 4.3 million jobs.[2] Moreover, in one of the most startling results of the 1980s, totally overlooked if not deliberately distorted in the passion-laden political debate, America's manufacturing productivity

TABLE 6–1
MANUFACTURING PRODUCTIVITY
IN SEVEN INDUSTRIALIZED COUNTRIES,
1960–1988 AND 1992–1993
(average annual rates of change)

	1960–73	1973–79	1979–88	1992	1993
United States	3.3	1.4	3.5	3.7	4.2
Canada	4.5	2.1	1.3	3.8	2.1
France	6.4	4.6	3.3	2.2	1.2
Germany	5.6	4.2	1.6	-0.8	2.3
Italy	6.4	5.7	4.1	4.8	6.3
Japan	10.2	5.0	4.0	-0.6	-0.6
United Kingdom	4.2	1.2	4.8	4.6	5.2

SOURCE: Bureau of Labor Statistics, U.S. Department of Labor.

soared from 1.4 percent per year from 1973 to 1979 to 3.5 percent per year from 1979 to 1988. Because productivity is the key constraint on real wages and living standards, this growth meant a dramatic improvement in real wages for more highly skilled American workers in the manufacturing sector, a 42 percent real increase over the full decade or about 3 percent per year.[3]

• Since manufacturing goods account for 70–80 percent of all goods traded in international markets, manufacturing productivity growth is the best measure of international trade competitiveness. By this measure, America's trade competitiveness in the 1980s did not decline but advanced. America gained on its industrial country competitors. By comparison, as table 6–1 shows, Germany's manufacturing productivity from 1979 to 1988 grew by less than half the rate of the United States or 1.6 percent per year; and in Europe, over the same period, only the United Kingdom (4.8 percent per year) and Italy (4.1 percent per year) exceeded America's gain. Japan's manufacturing productivity continued to grow at a clip of

4 percent per year but considerably down from 10 percent per year in the 1960s and 5 percent per year in the 1970s. Moreover, in 1992 and 1993, the latest years for which data are available, Japan's manufacturing productivity *dropped* by -0.6 percent per year, and Germany's dropped by -0.8 percent in 1992 before recovering to 2.3 percent in 1993. Meanwhile, U.S. manufacturing productivity rose strongly and steadily in both years by 3.7 percent and 4.2 percent, respectively.

• It is true that America's *relative* economic position in the world (in terms of share of GNP) declined after 1945 (the consequence of a deliberate policy that helped us gain a more friendly political world by sharing economic wealth, as discussed in chapter 2). But there is evidence that this convergence of other countries on the U.S. lead stopped in the 1980s, and no country is close to passing the United States in key indicators. In the early 1990s, the United States is still by far, in *absolute* terms, the most productive country in the world, which means it enjoys the highest real standard of living.[4] In 1990 Germany, France, Japan, and the United Kingdom had levels of *total* productivity or standards of living that reached only 85 percent or less of that of the United States and levels of *manufacturing* productivity that reached only 80 percent or less of the U.S. level. Even in individual manufacturing sectors, labor productivity in the United States exceeded that in Germany in seven of nine sectors and in Japan in four of nine.[5] In services, America's lead is even more impressive, and it is across-the-board in all sectors.[6] Europe and Japan have only begun to modernize their telecommunications, banking, insurance, airlines, and retail sectors. In the United States, in early 1994, 50 percent of all people in the work force had personal computers; in Japan the number was 14 percent. In the United States, 1.2 million computers were hooked up to the Internet; in Japan, 3,900.[7] Annual sales of personal computers in Europe are only one-half that in the United States.[8]

• All these improvements occurred despite the spiraling debt in the 1980s. U.S. government debt owed to the public soared from $1 trillion in 1980 to $3 trillion in 1992. (This figure excludes in 1992 about $1 trillion that the government owed itself.) Private debt soared as well. Consumer debt as a percentage of disposable income went from around 60 percent in 1980 to over 80 percent in 1994.[9] And the debt of nonfinancial corporations, measured by interest expense as a percentage of cash flow, rose from 21 percent in 1980 to 39 percent in 1990 before declining to 27 percent in 1992.[10] Much of this borrowing, because of the distorted macroeconomic conditions, went into consumption and waste, but not as much as the most caustic critics of the 1980s, such as Benjamin Friedman, contend.[11] Significant investments were made to spur the manufacturing productivity growth in American industry and to expand the service sector.

None of these data suggest that the period of the 1980s was a model decade for American economic policy. The accumulation of debt was broadly debilitating, and the dismal failure to moderate the budget deficit offset the successes in lowering inflation and revitalizing growth and productivity in American industry. But the record also does not justify the excessive pessimism that fuels the enthusiasm for interventionist trade and domestic industrial policies, particularly as it concerns America's trade competitiveness. Trade, as noted above, is mostly in manufactured goods, and America improved more in manufacturing sectors in the 1980s than any of its industrial nation rivals. During the 1980s, manufacturing productivity in Germany and Japan was on a downward path compared with the 1970s; America's manufacturing productivity was on an ascending path.

What about the argument that even if domestic macroeconomic policies were corrected, there would still be a need for strategic trade policy to meet the new, more competitive conditions of world trade markets? The answer to that argument is simple. Let us try it. Let us correct the macroeconomic problem, and then we will take a closer look at the indicators, such as trade deficits and the like, that might dictate further steps in the direction of strategic trade interventionism. My guess is that at that point strategic trade policy arguments, like infant industry arguments, would fall back into place and perspective. A few isolated cases of intervention may still be useful, especially with a difficult country such as Japan. But the broad enthusiasm for strategic trade policy, as an alternative to freer trade, would be exposed for what it is, an ideological position far less realistic than the proven experience over decades with freer trade.

7

A Broader Compass
for U.S. Trade Policy

Clinton administration trade policy is too narrowly conceived. It is separated from both traditional national security and domestic economic policy objectives. Yet it is called on both to lead American foreign policy into the new era of geo-economics and to be the cutting edge of domestic economic policy in the new information revolution at home. The goals trade policy has set for itself are far beyond its means for achieving.

Laura Tyson, director of the National Economic Council in the White House and former chairwoman of President Clinton's Council of Economic Advisers, exhibits the tendency to define U.S. trade policy in very narrow, specific terms.[1] She distinguishes herself from both traditional free traders (such as Jagdish Bhagwati) and moderate free traders (such as Lawrence Summers and Robert Reich, who are also in the Clinton administration), not because she disagrees with them that America's competitiveness problems are largely home-grown. Rather, she sets herself apart because, unlike traditional free traders, she believes that multilateral solutions to trade problems are a long way off and, unlike moderate free traders, she believes that in the interim targeting by foreign countries can hurt American firms in specific product areas affecting *what* as well as *how much* America sells. Hence, she develops a defensive policy of selective, sectoral retaliation to protect American firms in the medium term but practices this policy with great caution—what she calls "cautious activism"—so that it does not compromise her desire for multilateral solutions in the longer term.

There is admirable nuance to such a policy approach, but it also risks far more than it can hope to gain. It advocates a defensive retaliatory strategy to deter trade threats in the medium term, while hoping that such retaliation will not interfere with multilateral solutions in the future. It is equivalent to saying, in terms of traditional national security policy, that the United States will retaliate, selectively but probably increasingly, against incursions on American strategic interests in Europe or elsewhere, at the same time that it hopes through such retaliation to build a consensus for peace and better relations with rival countries. Defensive policies, whether security or trade policies, cannot achieve offensive goals. They can, at best, deter an adversary or, at worst, provoke it. They defend the status quo or make it worse. In trade policy, this is obviously important for analysts such as Tyson who believe the United States is falling behind daily in trade competitiveness. But, as I have just detailed, the evidence of such a decline is not persuasive.

What do "cautious activists" suggest for U.S. trade policy in the longer term? Precious little. They exhaust themselves addressing the sectoral trade policy issues and have little left to say about national security or traditional domestic policy considerations. They rely instead on a vague hope that once the United States gets tough, trading partners will "switch rather than fight." They offer these partners no broader national security purposes to open their markets, such as marshaling resources of industrial nations to support the transition to democracy in the former Communist world. And they underestimate the extent to which traditional macroeconomic solutions would reduce U.S. trade imbalances, particularly considering that America's trade imbalances are *not* primarily a consequence of flagging American trade (that is, manufacturing) competitiveness.

Strategic trade policy analysts are looking for the problem in the wrong place, namely at the sectoral level, and cannot be sure they have found a distortion at that level even when they think they have, because so many other factors could be causing the distortion. Moreover, their remedies, further sectoral intervention, are likely only to compound the distortions. They insist that they still favor multilateral goals, but they neither link sectoral retaliations to these goals (that is, link a semiconductor market access agreement to a multilateral agreement on competition and antitrust policies) nor offer any strategy for climbing out of the details of individual sector arrangements into the "blue skies" of cross-sectoral, multilateral bargains that might strengthen the trading system of the GATT and the WTO. Instead, they are ready to run up the flag of victory if they can show, amid mind-numbing assumptions, that a market access agreement raised sales by $1 billion and exports by $400 million. These figures represent the outer limits of the gains from the semiconductor agreement if one attributes all gains to the agreement, that is, as if nothing else happened that might have spurred sales, like an economic boom in Japan in the late 1980s.[2]

Trade policy cannot substitute for traditional national security or domestic economic policies. At best, trade policy is a complementary instrument. Military power and the domestic economy still count for much more in the equation of national security and prosperity. Thus, when trade policy is undercut by security and economic policies, it is severely weakened.

Strategic trade policy links trade to specific export and job targets but never links economic strength to actual military threats or broader economic objectives (such as global prosperity for reforming countries in Europe). Moreover, by promoting economic nationalism, it risks external retaliation and the creation of economic setbacks and potential military conflicts where none exists today. Strategic trade policy further separates trade advantage from stable prices and factor mobility and links it instead with manipulated prices (through subsidies, for instance) and to labor and capital market interventions on a sector-by-sector basis. In general, this approach complicates and actually impedes the successful management of macroeconomic policies, both by adding to government spending through subsidies and by creating greater rigidities at the microeconomic level, which weaken an economy's ability to adjust to competitive changes.

Weakened in this manner, strategic trade policy still promises much more. It promises more higher-paying jobs, more access to foreign markets, and ultimately more progress toward multilateral trade agreements. It cannot succeed, however, unless it gets more help from a broader framework of national security and domestic economic policy objectives.

None of the recommendations made here minimizes the necessity of tough bargaining with American trade partners. For this purpose, unilateral (like 301), bilateral (such as voluntary import expansions), and regional (NAFTA, for example) trade policy instruments will continue to be useful in selective cases, as they have been. They are not incompatible with global trade liberalization, but they must be guided by larger goals. They must be assisted by heavier weapons from the traditional national security and domestic economic policy arsenals. Strategic trade policy can apply in certain limited, specific circumstances, but it does not apply *generally,* and it does not provide a full-blown alternative rationale to freer trade. It can succeed only to the extent that free, open, and competitive markets continue to exist, as the experience of the Asian development model suggests. And free, competitive global markets can exist only to the extent that a political and national security rationale encourages openness as an expression of democratic tolerance and calls for efficient exchange and reallocation of resources to meet higher goals, such as helping the defeated countries of the cold war and reforming developing countries join the free world community.

Trade and Domestic Values

Trade policy is both an expression of a country's own domestic society and an instrument for safeguarding the security of that society. America practices freer trade because its domestic society favors consumers and freedom of choice and because open international markets add to transparency and tolerance in foreign relations. How far can America go in compromising its commitment to freer trade without restricting freedom at home and reducing tolerance abroad?

This is a serious question for strategic trade policy advocates who envy the producer-oriented economy of Japan and advocate accepting the corrupt, cartel-like practices of Japanese industry as a basis for managing world trade. Market sharing arrangements, in which an aggrieved party demands a specific share of a foreign market to compensate for past restrictions, have been compared with affirmative action programs.[3] It is a fair comparison. Jesse Jackson, speaking about blacks and affirmative action at home, told a conference in Minneapolis in July 1995 that "all we want from America is what America wants from Japan—a level playing field."[4] And Douglas Irwin, speaking about voluntary import expansion agreements with Japan, notes that these agreements in effect create an "entitlement" environment for favored firms or countries.[5] Usually, such entitlements are advocated by weaker parties, that is, noncompetitive firms or countries. In the 1970s, for example, the developing countries demanded a new international economic order, the purpose of which was to compensate them for the costs of colonization by setting up internationally managed markets. Now, according to strategic trade policy advocates, the United States is apparently the weaker party. It demands set-asides to compensate it for predatory Japanese behavior in semiconductors, automobiles, and other products. How far does this process go? Can any weaker party at any time claim redress? Do the Europeans or Japanese get to claim affirmative action programs to compensate them for earlier postwar American monopolies in aviation, nuclear power, and oil? Where does the victimization end? And who decides who is a victim? Strategic trade policy, at least when it is advocated from the standpoint of a victimized American industry suffering from "unfair" trade practices abroad, has much in common with the victimization theme in domestic politics. Victims take no responsibility for their own shortcomings; they blame others and look to governments for compensation. The market share approach to trade policy is a big brother or big government approach to politics. Clearly, freer trade and strategic trade are not just about foreign policy but about domestic choices concerning the proper role of government as well.

Managed trade involves domestic, not just international, constraints. Market shares have to be monitored; quotas have to be allocated. Admittedly, that goes on now in textiles, sugar, and the like. Do we want more? Managed trade is a back door to a managed economy. It favors those who already have status and power. Corporations in Japan and Germany exercise far more power over the lives of individuals in those countries than corporations do in America. So do technocrats. There is a decidedly statist and elitist bias to the managed-trade model. It is ironic indeed that just as country after country in the former Communist world and in the third world is casting off the shackles of statism, strategic trade policy analysts are asking Americans to try on more statism. Despite America's superior performance, they have no faith in a system of

99

individual choice. As one strategic trade advocate queries: "Can it be that the notion of individualism, so sacred to the United States, is also its fatal flaw?"[6]

Trade policy is about choice and freedom as well as jobs. In the rivalry among capitalisms, therefore, the choice between a producer- and a consumer-oriented economy is an important one. There are excesses in both—for example, unchecked consumer spending in the United States and forced savings in Japan. And convergence, as noted earlier, is taking place. But the issues are not just material; they are also moral. The type of trade policy America pursues expresses the type of society America is and wants to be.

America needs to have more confidence in its own social and economic model. The ethnic diversity and individual creativity of American society are totally incompatible with the ethnic homogeneity and authoritarian traditions of most Asian societies. The Asian model, as I have argued, succeeded only because it was embraced at the global level by the American model of openness and free trade. What is more, the Asian model is changing. To survive in the information age, Asian economies have to move into the services and globalize industrial production and trade. If they do not, they will remain followers. If they do change, their economies will take on characteristics more similar to other industrial nations. Asian markets will become truly open even as they become more innovative.

Trade and National Security

America's security is now inextricably linked to the fate of industrial nations in Europe and Asia. A good part of the Old World is now the New World—a free, democratic family of nations that resolve their differences through commerce, law, and republican governments. In an important sense, open societies and markets, albeit with different styles of capitalism, are an internal feature of all these countries and therefore also a characteristic of relations among them. Inevitably, economic competition and trade policy acquire a larger profile and generate more heat among these countries precisely because military power matters less. A certain hypersensitivity about trade issues therefore is to be expected. The United States and Europe have been fighting trade "wars" since the early 1960s, and the United States and Japan since the early 1970s. Such trade wars are not to be confused, however, with real wars. They occur precisely because there is less chance of real wars among industrial countries. Trade conflicts are a reflection of converging, not diverging, political relations. What is not to be expected or tolerated, therefore, is to lose perspective, pull trade relations out of context, declare that Japan and Germany are engaging in economic warfare,[7] and, because one expects once again full-scale military rivalry between the United States and its former allies,[8] advocate a drastic reconfiguration of America's security interests that ruptures America's relations with other democratic societies.

As this essay has argued, America's security interests cannot be met without a partnership with Europe and Japan. Nor, interestingly, can those of Europe and Japan. Today, Germany is the strongest supporter of NATO and its expansion to the East, knowing best the conflicts beyond its eastern border that could threaten continued European peace and prosperity. And Japan, because the end of the cold war left serious remaining conflicts in Asia such as the Northern Territories, China, North Korea, and so forth, "continues to need American support . . . more than America needs its Japanese ally in the absence of a hostile military and ideological superpower rival," namely the former Soviet Union.[9]

Even with the end of the cold war, therefore, the United States retains significant leverage from its security ties. It should exploit this leverage to push the allies toward greater openness and freer trade with the former Communist countries of Europe and the developing nations of Asia. The link is obvious. Just as the establishment of NATO could not have succeeded in the 1950s without the Marshall Plan, the expansion of NATO cannot succeed in the 1990s without a comparable and parallel economic initiative with Europe and Asia in the world economy and trading system. The president and secretary of state have to drive this point home at every opportunity. When they fail to do so, other countries get a free ride to reject American market-opening measures as instruments of American mercantilism. France objected to agricultural reforms in the recently completed GATT round because these reforms benefited American exports. In fact, the reforms benefited exports from the reforming countries of central and Eastern Europe much more. A broader security framework would make it harder for France (or the United States) to reject principled policies on petty commercial grounds, even though petty trade disputes will not necessarily go away.

Similarly, the economic promise of Asia cannot be realized without better security and political ties in the region. It is folly to think that a stable political basis exists in this region to support growing economic dynamism. The existing U.S.-Japan security treaty is fundamental to such security, but too narrow. From this foundation, the United States should seek to multilateralize political and security ties.[10] This process involves slowly converting bilateral security ties in the region (U.S.-Japan, U.S.-Korea) into multilateral ones, first a trilateral arrangement with Japan and South Korea and then a multilateral forum with other Asian nations (such as the members of ASEAN, the Association of Southeast Asian Nations), coordinating efforts to deal with a paranoid North Korea and an internally troubled China. Broader security discussions could go on at the same time with North Korea and China in the Asian Regional Forum (ARF). But ARF is little more than a confidence-building exercise. Real security in the region depends on alliances with South Korea and Japan and the possibility of wider multilateral, political reconciliation among America's friends in Asia.

Without a wider and stronger political community in Asia, economic ties in Asia rest on a very fragile foundation. What is more, these ties lead to continued excessive dependence on the U.S. market. The United States remains the principal market and engine for growth for practically all the Asian countries—first Japan, then the Four Tigers, now China. The United States runs substantial trade deficits with each of these countries.[11] The underlying reason for this bilateral burden in trade is the bilateral structure of security. Asian countries trust the United States more than they do each other. The U.S.-Japan Framework Agreement for bilateral trade issues, created by President Clinton in Tokyo in July 1993, only perpetuates this outmoded bilateral approach to Asian economic and political relations.

Trade and Real Bargaining Leverage

Critics may say that all this is well and good, but what if the allies just cool their heels? The United States has to provide security in Europe and Asia for its own interests; the allies can just free ride. Moreover, the allies increasingly reject freer trade. Their style of capitalism and society is less offended by the corporatism and anticonsumer bias of a world of strategic trade.

Ultimately, America has security leverage. In the post–cold war world, Europe and Japan need the United States more than the United States needs them. Their security is immediately affected by events in their regions, such as Bosnia and North Korea. U.S. interests are affected, too, but not as immediately. The United States could always hold back or withdraw, at least temporarily. Temporizing, however, as the United States is still doing in Bosnia in the summer of 1995, involves only negative and ultimately little leverage because the threat to stay out permanently is not credible. American negotiators need to look for more positive ways to use America's security leverage.

In Europe and Asia, the United States should take a stronger leadership role, not by getting more involved than its allies but by formulating a larger strategy that co-opts the allies and provides a consistent rationale for opening markets and expanding trade. In Europe, the United States and the EU should decide on a common date for membership of the central and Eastern European countries in both the EU and NATO.[12] The two organizations need to be expanded in tandem: they are not rivals, and neither can substitute for the other. The EU cannot provide security, especially nuclear security, for a long time to come, and a paper commitment by NATO is of little use if the central and Eastern European countries stall out economically because they do not have full access to the U.S. and European markets to strengthen their economies and ultimately their defense capabilities. The date for membership does not have to be soon, not because it might provoke the Russians but because the commitment is more important than the precise year. This framework would create the confidence to negotiate gradual, incremental steps toward full integration in security and economic relations with Western countries. Such steps would include trade liberalization with EU countries and a new round of global trade negotiations focused particularly on the needs of central and Eastern European countries (and other reforming countries in the developing world).

American leaders must make clear that a deepening of American defense commitments through NATO's expansion makes no sense unless America also deepens its economic ties to Europe. By expanding NATO without prompting European states toward new market-opening economic initiatives, the United States forfeits valuable leverage. It is even worse when the United States reacts coolly to proposals for new trade and economic initiatives that Europeans themselves suggest. In the spring of 1995, for example, several European leaders called for a free trade agreement between the United States and Europe.[13] The United States delayed and then reacted routinely to this suggestion. The idea of a transatlantic trade and economic initiative is far more consequential for American national interests than an automobile deal with Japan. But, in the cacophony of the automobile dispute, this idea was barely audible. U.S. trade policy is way off the mark when it fails to seize these opportunities to integrate security and economic initiatives.

Similarly, in the former Yugoslavia, the United States should integrate its security commitments with economic pressures. France wants the United States to put ground forces in Bosnia. France is also the primary obstacle to market-opening initiatives toward central and Eastern European states. The United States might consider increasing security commitments if France agrees to new economic initiatives. The United States need not put troops in Bosnia, but it might do so in Macedonia, where it already has modest forces. This step does not involve U.S. ground forces in the current war, but it clearly signals that the United States and its allies will not let the war widen to the north (Slovenia, Hungary) or the south (Macedonia, Greece). And if the United States is not ready to prevent a wider war, its Partnership for Peace program and NATO expansion to extend security protection to central Europe make no sense at all. What would we defend Hungary with if it became involved in a conflict with Serbia to protect Hungarian minorities in Voyvodina, the northern province of Serbia? Speeches?

In Asia, the United States has to move beyond the cold war structure of bilateral security agreements if it is going to build a political infrastructure that can sustain and nurture economic openness and growth. Japan remains the core element of a larger security structure, but Japan is currently isolated militarily in the region. The United States and Japan need to begin a process of political and military reconciliation with Japan's neighbors. This effort should start with South Korea. At present the two countries want nothing to do with one another militarily (unlike historical rivals, France and Germany, in Europe). This situation jeopardizes U.S. interests. As Chalmers Johnson and E.B. Keehn point out, "The Pentagon should ponder the specter of Japanese warships standing idly by while the United States takes major risks to defend South Korea."[14] How long would it take the U.S. Congress and public opinion, disillusioned by decades of bitter trade disputes with Japan, to pull the plug on a solo U.S. security role in Asia? The situation in the first Korean War is not likely to repeat itself. At that time, Japan was so weak it could not be expected to participate, and trade issues between the two countries did not exist. Political rapprochement among U.S. allies in Asia is an overriding imperative to sustain America's involvement in Asia. It will also do more to accelerate market openness within Asia than further bilateral trade agreements. Exclusively bilateral security ties in Asia have led to largely bilateral trade ties. The United States absorbs the brunt of export aggressiveness by all the rapidly growing Asian countries, from Japan, South Korea, and Taiwan in the past to mainland China today. Trade follows political community, and the ironic fact in Asia is that countries in the region have felt closer to the United States than to one another.

To persuade Japan and South Korea to work more closely together, the United States has to offer a wider plan for managing relations with China. Initial Clinton policies toward human rights and most-favored-nation treatment of China alienated Japan, even as the United States was negotiating vigorously to open the Japanese market (the framework talks). Today, Japan favors speedy entry of China in the new World Trade Organization, while the United States stonewalls until China adopts more acceptable trading rules. Again, a broad trade-off is possible that integrates security and economic interests. Japan agrees to multilateral security talks and exercises with South Korea to safeguard against a new threat from North Korea and political instability in China. The United States accepts Chinese membership in the WTO on somewhat softer technical grounds than it currently demands. Over time, a political reconciliation process, especially among South Korea, the three Chinas (mainland, Taiwan, and Hong Kong), and the ASEAN states, will do more to open markets within the region than bilateral trade leverage or formal WTO standards. The United States will no longer have to absorb a disproportionate share of exports from the region, and a viable multilateral security framework in the region will safeguard against a potentially dangerous political transition in China and future difficulties with North Korea.

Formulating a larger security and political strategy to advance U.S. trade interests in Europe and Asia does not mean that the United States has to give up its regional and bilateral trade negotiating leverage. U.S. policy should continue to promote NAFTA, APEC, and bilateral trade talks and, when necessary, take appropriate unilateral action. The problem with current measures to open foreign markets is that they stand alone. They get no support from traditional national security or domestic economic policies. A wider framework would assist, not detract from, trade objectives.

A frequent criticism of cold war policies is that the United States paid a price in the trade area to advance its security objectives. Except for an initial period at the outset of the cold war when the United States tolerated discrimination against its exports in Europe and, for much longer, in Japan, this criticism is totally false. U.S. cold war policies served not only U.S. security interests but also U.S. economic interests and built a powerful, liberalized, and integrated world economic community, which is today spreading to former adversary and developing countries alike. These policies created more competition, to be sure. But that competition was unquestionably the spur that led

America to restructure in the 1980s and keeps it from becoming complacent today. How can any of this be construed as contrary to America's trading interests?

A broader security framework is essential to support effective trade policies. Europe and Asia can be persuaded to open markets if the purpose, as they might see it, is not to satisfy American mercantilism in strictly bilateral deals but to enhance the prospects of reforms and prosperity in former Communist countries and China. Europe may be pressed to accept an earlier global trade round linked to the needs of the former Communist countries if the United States assumes a stronger and steadier leadership role in security issues in Europe, setting a common date with its allies for NATO and EU membership and taking steps to prevent a widening war in the Balkans. Japan and South Korea may begin a process of political reconciliation and mutual economic opening if the United States initiates a multilateral process of security talks to forge a common policy toward North Korea and China.

Specific trade negotiations may be linked to these larger developments. The United States might include South Korea in framework talks with Japan in certain sectors, such as semiconductors, where the United States and South Korea have common interests in gaining access to the Japanese market. Or regional trade negotiations in APEC might pick up negotiations in sectors left unfinished by the recent GATT round (such as financial services) and initiate representative agreements in new areas (an investment code, for example) that might be globalized in a subsequent WTO multilateral trade round.

Even bilateral and unilateral steps might be linked to larger objectives. A semiconductor agreement that is declared a "success" if Japan imports 20 percent of its domestic supplies sells U.S. leverage short. The agreement should call not only for a market share target (as long as it is open to all foreign suppliers) but also for progress toward harmonizing industrial policies in the electronics sector in the WTO. Such harmonization would eventually replace market share agreements with common rules. In past years, U.S. policy actually resisted the globalization of bilateral agreements. The United States rejected, for example, a European appeal to multilateralize the 1992 bilateral agreement on civil aircraft.[15] Unilateral actions, too, might involve links with larger objectives. If the United States is forced to retaliate in specific cases, it should link lifting sanctions to progress in multilateral as well as bilateral talks (for example, linking a 301 action to retaliate against procurement policies in Japan with progress toward more effective procurement codes in the WTO). This type of approach is actually tougher than those advocated by bilateral trade hawks and much more consequential.

No negotiating leverage is possible, however, if America continues to circumvent its budget deficit problem. To his credit, Clinton made an initial attempt in 1993 to close the budget gap. His package, however, did not inspire confidence. It fared no better politically than George Bush's package in 1990. The Democratic Party sustained an unprecedented congressional defeat in November 1994. In 1995, Clinton backed off the budget issue. The Republican Party, which now controls Congress, has taken the lead. Neither party can ignore politics, however, and the fact is that the three most serious efforts to cut the budget in the past ten years (1985, 1990, and 1993) were all followed by political defeats for the incumbent parties—the Republican Senate in 1986, George Bush in 1992, and the Democratic Congress in 1994. The prospects for overcoming these political obstacles are not likely to improve as a presidential election year approaches. This self-inflicted budget deadlock, more than any unfair trade practices in Japan or insufficient strategic trade interventions in the United States, cripples America's trade policy leverage.

America is squandering its trade leverage on limited deals in isolated sectors. Unconnected to traditional national security and domestic economic objectives, U.S.

trade policy languishes. A revitalization of effective trade leverage requires a larger perspective. If the United States invests more confidence in its own system, moves boldly to confront the domestic budget deficit, and exercises its security leadership and leverage in Europe and Asia, it can formulate a larger strategy that reconnects trade policy to essential national objectives, both abroad and at home. Trade policy would once again become truly strategic, and President Clinton might salvage and advance a trade policy that is slowly succumbing to the piranhas of protectionism.

Notes

CHAPTER 1: TRADE POLICY ADRIFT

1. See comments by Jeffrey Garten, under secretary of commerce for international trade, *New York Times*, May 14, 1995; and Michael McCurry, press secretary to the president, *New York Times*, May 17, 1995.

2. *Washington Post*, June 29, 1995. The auto dispute under George Bush produced numerical projections by Japanese automobile producers that they would increase auto parts purchases to $19 billion by March 31, 1995, a target that Japanese producers met. The 1995 agreement contained only general market projections by Japanese companies that did not indicate any specific numbers. U.S. officials estimated these numbers to be about $9 billion of additional parts purchases over three years, but the Japanese government explicitly stated in the agreement that it had no responsibility or obligations whatsoever in connection with these numbers.

3. Strategic trade policy in this essay refers to three broad sets of arguments: (1) the economic argument, popularized theoretically and then rejected practically by Paul Krugman (see *Strategic Trade Policy and the New International Economics* [Cambridge, Mass.: MIT Press, 1986]; and "Is Free Trade Passé?" *Economic Perspectives*, vol. 1, no. 2 [Fall 1987], pp. 131–44), that contemporary trade is no longer primarily a function of static factor endowments and comparative advantage that governments promote by withdrawing from the marketplace but rather a function of technological change, scale economies, and learning experience that governments influence through direct intervention in the marketplace; (2) the institutional argument that rival capitalist economic systems, particularly those in the United States and Japan, differ so greatly from one another that common multilateral rules for free trade are no longer possible and that trade negotiations and agreements have to be based on a bilat-

eral or plurilateral, results-oriented or quota system rather than the traditional multilateral price mechanism (see Clyde V. Prestowitz, Jr., *Trading Places* [New York: Basic Books, 1988]); and (3) the geostrategic argument that economic competition has replaced military rivalries in the post–cold war world and that the United States, therefore, can liberate its foreign economic policies from security or alliance constraints and pursue a much more self-interested policy of economic warfare with its former cold war allies (see Edward N. Luttwak, *The Endangered American Dream* [New York: Simon and Schuster, 1993]). While these arguments are not related or pursued in any consistent fashion by the Clinton administration, they do underlie a significant portion of the Clinton administration's thinking about trade policy and are advocated by some both inside and outside the administration as a broad, full-fledged alternative to traditional freer trade policies based on comparative advantage, multilateral rules, and alliance and security objectives. (*Freer trade* is used in this volume instead of *free trade* to indicate that U.S. trade policy during the cold war was never the pursuit of the ideal of free trade but the practical and progressive lowering of trade barriers amid significant and continuing roles for government in the U.S. and other economies.)

4. Mickey Kantor, the U.S. trade representative, writes in the introduction to the *1995 Trade Policy Agenda* released in March 1995 that the United States, "as a mature economy with *few domestic opportunities for growth,* . . . must reach the 96 percent of [its] customers who live outside the United States" (emphasis added).

5. Henry R. Nau, *The Myth of America's Decline* (New York: Oxford University Press, 1990).

6. Jeffrey E. Garten, *The Cold Peace: America, Japan, Germany, and the Struggle for Supremacy* (New York: Times Books, 1992).

7. Theodore H. Moran, *American Economic Policy and National Security* (New York: Council on Foreign Relations, 1993).

8. Laura D'Andrea Tyson, *Who's Bashing Whom? Trade Conflict in High Technology Industries* (Washington, D.C.: Institute for International Economics, 1992).

9. On the fallacy of comparing a country with a corporation, see Paul Krugman, "Competitiveness: A Dangerous Obsession," *Foreign Affairs,* vol. 73, no. 2 (March-April 1994), pp. 28–45.

10. See indictment of administration officials along these lines by Krugman in ibid. and responses of his critics in "The Fight over Competitiveness," *Foreign Affairs*, vol. 73, no. 4 (July-August 1994).

11. James M. Fallows, *Looking at the Sun: The Rise of the New East Asian Economies and Political Systems* (New York: Pantheon, 1994).

12. Jeffrey A. Hart, *Rival Capitalists: International Competitiveness in the United States, Japan, and Western Europe* (Ithaca, N.Y.: Cornell University Press, 1992).

13. Samuel P. Huntington, "Why International Primacy Matters," *International Security*, vol. 17, no. 4 (Spring 1993), pp. 68–84.

14. *Financial Times*, September 30, 1994.

15. McKinsey and Company, *Manufacturing Productivity* (Washington, D.C.: McKinsey Global Institute, October 1993), and *Service Sector Productivity* (Washington, D.C.: McKinsey Global Institute, October 1992.)

CHAPTER 2: TRADE AND NATIONAL SECURITY

1. Clyde V. Prestowitz, Jr., Ronald A. Morse, and Alan Tonelson, eds., *Powernomics: Economics and Strategy after the Cold War* (Washington, D.C.: Economic Strategy Institute, 1991).

2. Edward N. Luttwak, *The Endangered American Dream* (New York: Simon and Schuster, 1993).

3. Richard Rosecrance, *The Rise of the Trading State* (New York: Basic Books, 1986).

4. Shintaro Ishihara, *The Japan That Can Say No* (New York: Simon and Schuster, 1989).

5. U.S. General Accounting Office, *U.S. Business Access to Certain Foreign State-of-the-Art Technology*, GAO/NSIA-91-278, September 1991.

6. Tyson, *Who's Bashing Whom?*

7. Moran, *American Economic Policy and National Security.*

8. Ibid.

9. Bruce Russett, with William Antholis, Carol R. Ember, Melvin Ember, and Zeev Maoz, *Grasping the Democratic Peace: Principles for a Post Cold-War World* (Princeton, N.J.: Princeton University Press, 1993.)

10. Conflicts such as the one in Northern Ireland are eth-

nic conflicts and do not qualify as interstate rivalries in the same manner as former territorial disputes in Europe such as French-German conflicts over Alsace-Lorraine or German-Polish disputes over Pomerania, Silesia, and so forth.

11. Max Singer and Aaron Wildavsky, *The Real World Order: Zones of Peace/Zones of Turmoil* (Chatham, N.J.: Chatham House Publishers, 1993).

12. John Lewis Gaddis, *The Long Peace: Inquiries into the History of the Cold War* (New York: Oxford University Press, 1987).

13. Henry R. Nau, "Rethinking Economics, Politics and Security in Europe," in *Reshaping Western Security*, ed. Richard N. Perle (Washington, D.C.: AEI Press, 1991).

14. Kenneth N. Waltz, *Theory of International Politics* (New York: McGraw-Hill, 1979).

15. Robert Gilpin, *War and Change in World Politics* (Cambridge, U.K.: Cambridge University Press, 1981).

16. Henry R. Nau, *At Home Abroad: American Foreign Policy in the Twenty-first Century*, forthcoming.

17. Charles P. Kindleberger, "Dominance and Leadership in the International Economy," *International Studies Quarterly*, vol. 25, no. 3 (June 1981), pp. 242–54.

18. Nau, *The Myth of America's Decline*.

CHAPTER 3: SECURITY THREATS AND TRADE INTERESTS

1. As the Clinton administration's Department of Defense report on *United States Security Strategy for the East Asian-Pacific Region* (February 1995, p. 15) puts it: "China's military modernization effort is in an early stage, and its long-term goals are unclear . . . . Absent a better understanding of China's plans, capabilities and intentions, other Asian nations may feel a need to respond to China's growing military power."

2. Garten, *The Cold Peace*.

3. For an analysis that reaches similar conclusions on economic grounds, see Claude E. Barfield, *The United States and East Asia: Trade, Investment and the Emergence of New Policies,* Paper prepared for the International Trade Project, American Enterprise Institute, 1995, p. 107.

4. For a useful perspective on this question, see Roy H. Ginsberg, "Principles and Practice of the European Union's

Common Foreign and Security Policy: Retrospective on the First Eighteen Months," Paper prepared for workshop sponsored by American Institute for Contemporary German Studies, U.S. Army War College, and Delegation of the Commission of the European Union, Washington, D.C., May 10, 1995.

5. Stanley R. Sloan, "European Proposals for a New Atlantic Community," CRS Report for Congress, Congressional Research Service, Library of Congress, 95-374S, March 1995.

6. John J. Mearsheimer, "Back to the Future: Instability in Europe after the Cold War," *International Security,* vol. 15, no. 4 (Spring 1990), pp. 5–57.

7. Dominique Moisi and Michael Mertes, "Europe's Map, Compass and Horizon," *Foreign Affairs,* vol. 74, no. 1 (January-February 1995), pp. 122–35.

8. Shafiqul Islam and Michael Mandelbaum, eds., *Making Markets: Economic Transformation in Eastern Europe and the Post-Soviet States* (New York: Council on Foreign Relations, 1993).

9. Gutam Naik, "Western Investment in Eastern Europe Grew Sharply in Recent Period," *Wall Street Journal,* October 4, 1993.

10. Rogers Brubaker, *Citizenship and Nationhood in France and Germany* (Cambridge, Mass.: Harvard University Press, 1992).

11. Fallows, *Looking at the Sun.*

12. See *New York Times,* November 21, 1993; and John Bresnan, *From Dominoes to Dynamos: The Transformation of Southeast Asia* (New York: Council on Foreign Relations, 1994).

13. Dennis J. Encarnation, *Rivals beyond Trade: America versus Japan in Global Competition* (Ithaca, N.Y.: Cornell University Press, 1992).

14. Barfield, *The United States and East Asia.*

15. Chalmers Johnson, *MITI and the Japanese Miracle* (Stanford, Calif.: Stanford University Press, 1982); Clyde V. Prestowitz, Jr., *Trading Places* (New York: Basic Books, 1988); and Fallows, *Looking at the Sun.*

16. Jagdish Bhagwati, *The World Trading System at Risk* (Princeton, N.J.: Princeton University Press, 1991).

17. Ibid., p. 66.

18. See Jagdish Bhagwati, "U.S. Trade Policy: The Infatuation with Free Trade Agreements," in *The Dangerous Obsession with Free Trade Areas,* by Jagdish Bhagwati and Anne O. Krueger (Washington, D.C.: AEI Press, 1995).

19. Barfield, *The United States and East Asia.*

CHAPTER 4: ALLEGED OBSTACLES TO TRADE

1. Michael E. Porter, *The Competitive Advantage of Nations* (New York: Free Press, 1990).

2. Michael Mastanduno, "Do Relative Gains Matter? America's Response to Japanese Industrial Policy," *International Security,* vol. 16 (Summer 1991), pp. 73–113.

3. James Kurth, "Things to Come: The Shape of the New World Order," *The National Interest,* no. 24 (Summer 1991), pp. 3–13.

4. Zbigniew Brzezinski, "A Plan for Europe," *Foreign Affairs,* vol. 74, no. 1 (January-February 1995), pp. 26–43.

5. Brubaker, *Citizenship and Nationhood in France and Germany.*

6. Fallows, *Looking at the Sun,* p. 167.

7. Christopher Wood, *The End of Japan Inc.* (New York: Simon and Schuster, 1994). See also Bill Emmott, *Japanophobia: The Myth of the Invincible Japanese* (New York: Times Books, 1992).

8. C. Fred Bergsten and Marcus Noland, *Reconcilable Differences? United States–Japan Economic Conflict* (Washington, D.C.: Institute for International Economics, June 1993), p. 42. On the savings surge in the United States, see Lowell Bryan and Diana Farrell, analysts at McKinsey and Company, "The Savings Surge," *Wall Street Journal,* November 7, 1994.

9. Pietro S. Nivola, *Regulating Unfair Trade* (Washington, D.C.: Brookings Institution, 1993), p. 93.

10. Lester Thurow, *Head to Head: The Coming Economic Battle among Japan, Europe and America* (New York: William Morrow and Company, Inc., 1992).

11. To appreciate the magnitude of this bill, imagine the U.S. Congress passing a bill to eliminate seats for incumbent members. In the United States, such redistricting is done every ten years on the basis of census figures by *state* legislatures and often subsequent court decisions.

12. Robin Gaster and Clyde Prestowitz, *Shrinking the Atlantic: Europe and the American Economy* (Washington, D.C.: North Atlantic Research, Inc., and Economic Strategy Institute, 1994).

13. Tyson, *Who's Bashing Whom?*

14. Thurow, *Head to Head.*

15. Theodore Moran and David C. Mowery, "Aerospace and National Security in the Era of Globalization," Consortium on Competitiveness and Cooperations working paper 91-2, Center for Research in Management, Berkeley, Calif.: University of California, 1991.

16. Kenneth Flamm, *Creating the Computer: Government, Industry and High Technology* (Washington, D.C.: Brookings Institution, 1988); and Dieter Ernst and David O'Connor, *Competing in the Electronics Industry—The Experience of New Industrializing Economies* (London: Pinter, 1992).

17. Henry R. Nau, *National Politics and International Technology: Nuclear Reactor Developments in Western Europe* (Baltimore, Md.: Johns Hopkins University Press, 1974).

18. Organization for Economic Cooperation and Development, *Technology and Globalization* (Paris: OECD, 1990).

19. Ernst and O'Connor, *Competing in the Electronics Industry.*

20. Nivola, *Regulating Unfair Trade,* p. 32.

21. McKinsey and Company, *Manufacturing Productivity,* Computer Section, p. 12.

22. Linda R. Cohen and Roger C. Noll, *The Technology Pork Barrel* (Washington, D.C.: Brookings Institution, 1991).

23. Tyson, *Who's Bashing Whom?,* p. 41.

24. Jagdish Bhagwati, *Protectionism* (Cambridge, Mass.: MIT Press, 1989), p. 97.

25. Nivola, *Regulating Unfair Trade,* p. 161.

26. Organization for Economic Cooperation and Development, *Historical Statistics, 1960–1990* (Paris: OECD, 1992).

27. Masaru Yoshitomi, "Developing New International Division of Labor in East Asia and Building a New U.S.-Pacific Asia Relationship," Paper prepared for the International Trade Project, American Enterprise Institute, 1995.

28. "Japan: The Wheezing Giant," *Investor's Business Daily,* July 3, 1995, p. B1.

29. "Slow Crisis in Japan," *Financial Times,* July 1–2, 1995, p. 8.

30. William Dawkins, "Trapped in a Dream World," *Financial Times,* July 5, 1995, p. 13.

31. See McKinsey and Company, *Service Productivity,* various sector studies.

32. Jonathon Sapsford, "Tokyo Concedes Broader Banking Crisis," *Wall Street Journal,* June 7, 1995.

33. See "Japan," *Financial Times Survey,* July 10, 1995; and

James Sterngold, "Japanese Rush to Sell Their U.S. Real Estate," *New York Times,* June 9, 1995.

34. See James K. Glassman, "Some Godzilla," *Washington Post,* June 27, 1995; Robert J. Samuelson, "They Have Met the Market—and Lost," *Washington Post,* March 20, 1995.

35. McKinsey and Company, *Manufacturing Productivity,* p. 3.

36. Robert Wade, "East Asia's Economic Success: Conflicting Perspectives, Partial Insights, Shaky Evidence," *World Politics,* vol. 44, no. 2 (January 1992), pp. 297–99.

37. Ibid., pp. 296–300.

38. Robert Wade, *Governing the Market: Economic Theory and the Role of Government* (Princeton, N.J.: Princeton University Press, 1990).

39. Henry R. Nau, "National Policies for High Technology Development and Trade: An International and Comparative Assessment," in *National Policies for Developing High Technology Industries,* ed. Francis W. Rushing and Carole Ganz Brown (Boulder, Colo.: Westview Press, 1986), p. 14.

40. Paul Krugman, "The Myth of Asia's Miracle," *Foreign Affairs,* vol. 73, no. 6 (November-December 1994), p. 78.

41. For a view that portrayed these investments as a threat to American security, see Martin and Susan Tolchin, *Buying into America* (New York: Times Books, 1988).

42. Bergsten and Noland, *Reconcilable Differences?* pp. 129–43.

43. Tyson, *Who's Bashing Whom?* p. 117.

44. Bergsten and Noland, *Reconcilable Differences?* p. 132.

45. Tyson, *Who's Bashing Whom?* p. 112.

46. Douglas A. Irwin, *Managed Trade: The Case against Import Targets* (Washington, D.C.: AEI Press, 1994), p. 58.

47. Tyson, *Who's Bashing Whom?* p. 140.

48. See Robert Z. Lawrence, "Efficient or Exclusionist? The Import Behavior of Japanese Corporate Groups," Brookings papers on economic activity, no. 1, 1991, pp. 311–30; Bergsten and Noland, *Reconcilable Differences?* p. 183; and Irwin, *Managed Trade,* pp. 40–50.

CHAPTER 5: TRADE AND DOMESTIC POLICIES

1. Robert Kuttner, *The End of Laissez-Faire* (New York: Alfred A. Knopf, 1991).

2. John Gerald Ruggie, "International Regimes, Transactions, and Change: Embedded Liberalism in the Post War Economics Order," in *International Regimes*, ed. Stephen D. Krasner (Ithaca, N.Y.: Cornell University Press, 1983).

3. Nau, *The Myth of America's Decline*. For a similar interpretation of economic policies before and after World War II, see Alan Brinkley, *The End of Reform: New Deal Liberalism in Recession and War* (New York: Alfred A. Knopf, 1995).

4. I.M. Destler, *American Trade Politics*, 2d rev. ed. (Washington, D.C.: Institute for International Economics, 1995).

5. White House, *A National Security Strategy of Engagement and Enlargement*, July 1994.

CHAPTER 6: AMERICA'S COMPETITIVENESS IN THE 1980s

1. William J. Baumol, Sue Anne Bater Blackman, and Edward N. Wolff, *Productivity and American Leadership: The Long View* (Cambridge, Mass.: MIT Press, 1989).

2. Edward Balls, "A Tide That's Not for Turning," *Financial Times*, January 9, 1993.

3. *Economic Report of the President* (Washington, D.C.: Government Printing Office, 1992), p. 97.

4. One should not be deceived by recent revisionist tendencies to place Japan's GDP per capita at 40–50 percent above that of the United States. This datum is pure illusion derived from the strong appreciation of the yen. The revisionists, who also argue, correctly in this case, that Japanese prices are systematically higher than those in the United States, cannot have it both ways. If domestic prices are higher and the yen is overvalued, Japan's real standard of living, in terms of purchasing power, is still well below that of the United States. See Clyde Prestowitz, Jr., "Premature Obituary on Japan's Economy," *Washington Post*, April 14, 1995.

5. McKinsey and Company, *Manufacturing Productivity*.

6. McKinsey and Company, *Service Sector Productivity*.

7. "1994 Round Table," *Barrons*, January 17, 1994.

8. Kyle Pope, "Europe's PC Business Increased 28.8% in 1st Period," *Wall Street Journal*, May 12, 1995, p. B2.

9. *Economic Report of the President*, 1994, p. 55.

10. L. Douglas Lee and Marlene Grabau, "Economics from

Washington," Research Report from Washington Analysis, A Division of Natwest Securities, February 8, 1993, p. 15.

11. Benjamin M. Friedman, *Day of Reckoning: The Consequences of American Economic Policy under Reagan and After* (New York: Random House, 1988).

CHAPTER 7: A BROADER COMPASS

1. Tyson, *Who's Bashing Whom?*
2. Bergsten and Noland, *Reconcilable Differences?* p. 136.
3. Prestowitz, *Trading Places*, p. 14.
4. "They're Looking for Justice—Justice Thomas," *Washington Post*, July 14, 1995.
5. Irwin, *Managed Trade*, p. 59.
6. Prestowitz, *Trading Places*, p. 14.
7. Huntington, "Why International Primacy Matters," p. 75.
8. See Paul Kennedy, *The Rise and Fall of the Great Powers* (New York: Random House, 1987), p. 338, for his predictions about Japan.
9. Bergsten and Noland, *Reconcilable Differences?* p. 13.
10. See Patrick M. Cronin and Michael J. Green, *Redefining the U.S.-Japan Alliance*, Institute for National Strategic Studies, National Defense University, McNair Paper 31, November 1994; and Joseph S. Nye, Jr., "East Asian Security: The Case for Deep Engagement," *Foreign Affairs*, vol. 74, no. 4 (July-August 1995), pp. 90–103.
11. In 1991, the U.S. market still accounted for 29.3 percent of Japan's exports, 26.4 percent of South Korea's, 29.3 percent of Taiwan's, 22.6 percent of Hong Kong's, 19.7 percent of Singapore's, 35.6 percent of the Philippines and 8.6 percent of China's. See Barfield, *The United States and East Asia*.
12. NATO is set to decide on enlargement by the end of 1995. The European Union has put off further enlargement decisions until after the Intergovernmental Conference in 1996.
13. Sloan, "European Proposals for a New Atlantic Community."
14. See "East Asian Security: The Pentagon's Ossified Strategy," *Foreign Affairs*, vol. 74, no. 4 (July-August 1995), p. 109.
15. Tyson, *Who's Bashing Whom?* p. 209.

About the Author

HENRY R. NAU is professor of political science and international affairs at George Washington University. He was assoicate dean at GWU's Elliott School of International Affairs from 1988 to 1992 and previously taught at Williams College and as a visiting professor at Stanford, Johns Hopkins, and Columbia Universities. He also served in the State Department from 1975 to 1977 as an international affairs fellow of the Council on Foreign Relations and in the White House from 1981 to 1983 as a senior staff member of the National Security Council. His books include *The Myth of America's Decline* (1990) and *National Politics and International Technology* (1974). He is completing a new book tentatively entitled *At Home Abroad: American Foreign Policy in the Twenty-first Century.*